The University of Alabama Press
Tuscaloosa, AL 35487-0380



***Theater History Studies*** is an official journal of the Mid-America Theatre Conference, Inc. (MATC). The conference encompasses the states of Illinois, Indiana, Iowa, Kansas, Michigan, Minnesota, Missouri, Nebraska, North Dakota, South Dakota, and Wisconsin. Its purposes are to unite people and organizations within this region and elsewhere who have an interest in theatre and to promote the growth and development of all forms of theatre.



***Theatre History Studies*** is devoted to research in all areas of theatre history. Manuscripts should be prepared in conformity with the guidelines established in the *Chicago Manual of Style,* submitted in duplicate, and sent to Rhona Justice-Malloy, Editor, Dept. of Theatre Arts, Isom Hall 110, University of Mississippi, Box 1848, University, MS 38677-1848 or by e-mail to rjmalloy@olemiss.edu. Consulting editors review the manuscripts, a process that takes approximately four months. The journal does not normally accept studies of dramatic literature unless there is a focus on actual production and performance. Authors whose manuscripts are accepted must provide the editor with an electronic file, using Microsoft Word. Illustrations (preferably high-quality originals or black-and-white glossies) are welcomed. Manuscripts will be returned only if accompanied by a stamped, self-addressed envelope bearing sufficient postage.

This publication is issued annually by the Mid-America Theatre Conference and The University of Alabama Press.

Subscription rates for 2008 are $15 for individuals, $30 for institutions, and an additional $8 for foreign delivery. Back issues are $29.95 each. Subscription orders and changes of address should be directed to Allie Harper, The University of Alabama Press, Box 870380, Tuscaloosa, AL 35487 (205-348-1564 phone, 205-348-9201 fax).

***Theatre History Studies*** is indexed in *Humanities Index, Humanities Abstracts, Book Review Index, MLA International Bibliography, International Bibliography of Theatre, Arts & Humanities Citation Index, IBZ International Bibliography of Periodical Literature,* and *IBR International Bibliography of Book Reviews,* the database of *International Index to the Performing Arts.* Full texts of essays appear in the databases of both *Humanities Abstracts Full Text* and *SIRS.* The journal has published its own index, *The Twenty Year Index, 1981–2000.* It is available for $10 for individuals and $15 for libraries from Rhona Justice-Malloy, Editor, Dept. of Theatre Arts, Isom Hall 110, University of Mississippi, Box 1848, University, MS 38677-1848.

**MID-AMERICA THEATRE CONFERENCE**

The Mid-America Theatre Conference is a regional affiliate of the American Theatre Association and encompasses the states of Iowa, Kansas, Minnesota, Nebraska, North Dakota, and South Dakota. Its purposes are to unite persons and organizations within the region with an interest in theatre and to promote the growth and development of all forms of theatre.

réamhrá vorwort prooemium предисловие

πρόλογος prefatory note prakalba

forord bevezetés esipuhe przedmowa

woord vooraf proemio avertissement předmluva

This issue of *Theatre History Studies* includes three articles first delivered as papers at the Third Annual Theatre History Symposium "Crosscurrents: The Art of the Theatre" at the Mid-America Theatre Conference held at the University of Iowa in March of this year. Several papers from the Symposium will appear in a future issue of *Theatre History Studies*. The journal will continue to publish selected manuscripts submitted directly to the publication and selected Symposium papers. All articles are refereed by at least two persons in the respective research area who, in some instances, may not necessarily be regular consulting editors.

The topic for the Fourth Annual Theatre History Symposium to be held March 16-18, 1984, at the Mid-America Theatre Conference in Omaha, Nebraska, will be "Shakespeare Production: Acting, Directing, and Staging." Session topics include: "British Productions of Shakespeare Prior to 1900," "Film Adaptations of Shakespeare," "The Production of Shakespeare's Plays in North America, 1875 to 1950: Contemporary Perspectives on Modern Practice," "Shakespeare in Germany and Eastern Europe," "Shakespeare in the Romance and Slavic Languages," "Contemporary Productions of Shakespeare in the U.S., 1946-Present," and "British Productions of Shakespeare Since 1900." Symposium coordinator is Harold J. Nichols at Kansas State University. Addresses for session coordinators are listed on page 141. The editors of *Theatre History Studies* cordially invite national and international theatre historians to participate in this unique opportunity for scholarly exchange.

The Mid-America Theatre Conference will sponsor a $400 award for a graduate student history research paper from the MATC seven state region to be presented at the 1984 Theatre History Symposium and subsequently published in *Theatre History Studies*. Oscar Brockett, University of Texas, Milly Barranger, University of North Carolina, and Richard Moody, Indiana University, will serve as the selection panel. Further information on page 141.

*Theatre History Studies* would like to welcome William Kuhlke, Professor of Theatre (Slavic Area) at the University of Kansas, to our Editorial Board. We also welcome two additional consulting editors, Denis Salter, University of Calgary, and Judith Milhous, University of Iowa.

The two photographic essays in this issue are the result of an expansion of the feature section "Theatre History Obscurities" to include more descriptive information concerning the historical item or document. I urge theatre historians and archivists to submit proposals.

Circulation of *THS* continues to grow. I thank those who have recommended the journal to their library and encourage others to do so. I am most appreciative for the undaunted dedication and professionalism of the editorial board members, Weldon Durham, William Kuhlke, Felicia Londré, Tice Miller, and Harold Nichols. I would like to commend Kent Neely for his sensitivity and leadership as CRO of the Mid-America Theatre Conference. Once again, I am grateful for the support extended by Bruce C. Jacobsen.

Ron Engle

# THEATRE HISTORY STUDIES

VOLUME III

## CONTENTS

1983

# Evgenii Bogrationovich Vakhtangov
## 1883-1922

*Evgenii Bogrationovich Vakhtangov was born in Vladikavkaz February 1, 1883. He died just thirty-nine years later, May 31, 1922. In his brief career as actor and especially as director he created an artistic legacy which continues to enrich our theatrical culture today as it has for over sixy years. His productions of* The Dybbuk *at the Habima and* Turandot *at his own Third Studio of the Moscow Art Theatre are bench marks in the struggle of modern Russian theatre to ascend to the expressive heights of Meierkhol'd's theatricalism without jetisoning its soul of Stanislavskiian inner realism. Furthermore, the actor training and rehearsal techniques which produced these works, especially* Turandot, *have inspired theatre artists far beyond the Soviet Union and now more than ever. Whenever we use the now ubiquitous techniques of action analysis and improvisation to train actors or to work on scenes, we are profiting from the wealth of Vakhtangov's legacy, and whenever we succeed in creating vividly expressive forms filled with powerfully affective inner belief, we repay in kind a little of the debt we owe to one of the artists who showed us the way. So rather than grieving once again over his untimely death, we choose with this edition of* Theatre History Studies *to celebrate the birth, one-hundred years ago, of one of the great innovators of the modern theatre.*

—WILLIAM KUHLKE

# Richard Mansfield's Production of *Richard the Third:* The Brave Finale to a Disappointing London Venture

C. ALEX PINKSTON, JR.

The career of American actor-manager Richard Mansfield (1854-1907) was distinguished in several respects. He embodied characteristics of earlier nineteenth century star actors: he possessed a flamboyant personality and displayed a distinctive style of acting in a large repertoire which he toured throughout the United States. Mansfield also helped usher in the twentieth century theatre: he performed in long-run engagements in New York and Chicago, emphasized psychological motivation in his acting, directed his own productions, championed American playwriting, and promoted the establishment of a National theatre. Mansfield experimented with original, untried scripts (Clyde Fitch's *Beau Brummel*, Bernard Shaw's *Arms and the Man* and *The Devil's Disciple*), theatrical adaptations of novels (*Dr. Jekyll and Mr. Hyde, The Scarlett Letter*), and theatrical treatments of the lives of famous historical characters (Napoleon and Nero). But he also produced classical works such as Shakespeare's *Richard III, The Merchant of Venice, Henry V* and *Julius Caesar;* Moliere's *The Misanthrope;* Schiller's *Don Carlos;* Tolstoi's *Ivan the Terrible;* and Ibsen's *Peer Gynt*. In all these renderings, modern and classical, Mansfield's chief concern was to create a highly artistic product. In his stagings of Shakespeare, however, and particularly in his staging of *Richard III* in London in 1889, the actor-manager's artistry reached its peak.

In the summer of 1888 Mansfield was a rising young star in the American theatre. Five years earlier he had scored a sudden triumph in New York as the Baron Chevrial in *A Parisian Romance*. During the 1886 and 1887 seasons he had starred in two new, immensely successful plays, *Prince Karl* and *Dr. Jekyll and Mr. Hyde,* and had written and starred in a third entitled *Monsieur*. Henry Irving was conducting one of his several American tours in 1888, and from every corner he heard of the young genius whose rise had been meteoric. After viewing Mansfield's acting in *Dr. Jekyll and Mr. Hyde,* Irving invited the young actor to come to London and appear at the Lyceum Theatre. Flattered beyond measure, Mansfield accepted Irving's terms, and on August 4, 1888 opened his London engagement with *Dr. Jekyll and Mr. Hyde,* then followed that run with productions of *A Parisian Romance* and *Prince Karl*. Although Mansfield received the London critics' praise, he did not win the London public's heart; attendance at each of these productions slacked after the novelty wore off. The Lyceum season, while

C. Alex Pinkston is Assistant Professor of Theatre Arts at Marquette University.

it enlarged his renown and prestige as an actor, left him heavily in debt to Henry Irving.[1] Although he was dissatisfied, depressed and physically weakened by the Lyceum season, Mansfield refused to lose heart. To prove himself Henry Irving's equal as an actor-manager, he elected to embark on another and more difficult venture: to act in London in one of the great plays of Shakespeare. To this end, he hired the Globe Theatre and began preparations for *Richard III*.

Mansfield's article, "The Story of a Production,"[2] contains Mansfield's personal notes taken during preparations for *Richard III*. It also captures the actor's frame of mind during this period and serves as an account of his intentions for the production. Tired out by his disappointing Lyceum engagement, Mansfield elected to remain in London just long enough to get the production underway, then formalize his interpretation of Gloster while recuperating in the country. He engaged Seymour Lucas, who had been his instructor some fifteen years earlier when Mansfield had studied painting in London, and together they developed designs for the costumes and armor. Mansfield, Lucas, and a bevy of scenic artists, which included William Telbin, Walter Hahn, E.G. Banks, and Bruce Smith, collaborated on scenic designs. Following the traditional nineteenth century "Theatre of Illusion," Mansfield determined to display the Plantagenet society on stage in magnificent historic settings, properties, costumes, armor and heraldic devices. But, for Mansfield, detailed realism was not an end in itself. While he affirmed that archaeological accuracy in staging would instruct the public in period dress and manners, he was far more concerned that the scenery, costumes, lighting and music create appropriate dramatic moods for the play's action.

Mansfield made the sketches for most of the play's scenes. His comments regarding the settings reveal that, although he was first an actor, Mansfield was clearly a scenic artist of the first order; and he envisioned the play's settings as atmospheric environments for the characters and action. For the first scene, the Tower of London, he determined to employ bright calciums to create the light of morning, "that pale white light that gives atmosphere and mystery, and lifts the towers higher, throws deeper shadows into angles, and helps the eye to imagine the black waters of the moat, the grim teeth of the portcullis, the little door in the warden's tower, and walls and yards, drawbridge and battlements — real, all real." For King Henry's chamber in the Tower he elected to construct a groined roof and pillared walls of rough stone. Into a recess he placed the King's bed, with a little window at the back of the bed and "a feeble ray of light straggling through on to the King's book; the oratory, with a large stained-glass window and the prie dieu and crucifix, and an ancient lamp flickering above; an all-prevailing idea of gloom and approaching horror." Mansfield contrasted this dark picture with one of "dancing life and light": the road to Chertsey where Richard woos Anne. He envisioned

> *flowers all abloom, the fields intersected by hedges white with May blossom, a bank where the silver-birch bend their graceful limbs over tangled grass and fern that hint of hidden violets and*

> *primroses, and the bold brush flashing a patch of brilliant yellow here and there. This in the middle distance: the fields stretching back in the blue summer haze to the roofs and towers of old London in the background. Further foreward a farm-house, with straw-thatched roof, green with lichen and ivy, as is the broken wall near the foreground, a carpet of grass at its foot and another birch nestling up against its back, buttercups and daisies growing at its foot, and the deep-rutted road winding across between farm-house on the right and cottage on the left. All shall be brilliant with an atmosphere that vibrates in the summer sunshine, and makes you long to lie back on the grass, and hark for the note of the lark out of sight up in the gray-blue.*[3]

With a painter's sensitivity, Mansfield imagined details which were picturesque and evocative.

The hall and throne room interiors of the middle acts Mansfield left to his designers. But he was adamant that Richard's camp in Act V be a departure from accepted and traditional handling. The tent would be on the extreme left and would not occupy the entire stage. The background would be "a low lying, bleak country, broken here and there by storm-torn willow and pools fringed with reeds, visited by the drifting clouds and the uncertain moon, the brown tents in the dip of the land, and the glow of the red camp fires here and there; far beyond, the watch-fires of Richmond's army by the line of indigo hills, and over their brow the lingering remembrance of the sun." Around the fire, said Mansfield, would be some knights, armed cap-a-pie, and the firelight caressing their burnished steel. The hum of both armies and the "clink of hammer closing rivets up" would give "dreadful note of preparation."[4] Mansfield displayed a cinematic eye in that he viewed the play's action in vivid pictures, invented realistic locales for the stage, and determined a specific atmosphere for each locale.

Mansfield's last two tasks in London were to complete a personal adaptation of Shakespeare's play and to engage Walter Pollock and Egerton Castle to supervise battle choreography. Having set the wheels in motion, the actor journeyed to Bournemouth, where he could study, receive communications and reports, and issue instructions. Edward German, one of the Lyceum composer-conductors, joined Mansfield there, and the two collaborated on a musical score. But most of his time in the country Mansfield spent developing, through his imagination, the life of the character he was to portray.

Mansfield made three significant decisions regarding Richard's character during his preliminary work on the role in the country, and these he published in the preface to his acting text. First, he determined to contrast Richard at nineteen in Act I and Richard at thirty-three in Act V to express the psychological terrors resulting from his progression in evil. Second, he subdued Richard's physical deformities and concentrated on the deformity of his mind. He cited historical evidence that Richard was an attractive young man, and he asserted that his own make-up and costumes were copied from historical portraits at Windsor, Eton, and the National Gallery. The deformity of Richard's mind, he explained, could best be motivated by revealing an increasing malignity of mind as Richard matured. He sought to contrast "Richard in his earlier and more careless days (his strength, his vast ambition, his imperial mind and reckless courage all fresh in him) with the haggard, conscience-stricken and careworn tyrant Shakespeare paints him fourteen years later."[5] Mansfield's final concern was to stress the triumph of Richard's pure intellect over extremely formidable obstacles. And he sought to stress Richard's motives by allowing the audience to glimpse moments of thought and decision prior to action.

While on retreat at Bournemouth the actor's imagination invented specific staging and pieces of business for himself and for other members of the cast. As he explains, "each movement of king, queen or pawn . . . passed in my mind. I knew where every one should go, where everyone should work."[6] He offered, as an example, his imagined playing of the moment of waking from the nightmare in the tent scene. When Catesby appears to Richard after his evil dream, says Mansfield, "I had mistaken him for another phantom, and thrown my sword away and crossed myself, and touched him and found him human, and thrown mine arms about him in an ecstasy of relief a thousand times." Mansfield invented such business in his imagination for each scene in the play. "I act them out and see myself doing them just as fully as if I actually moved my body and wagged my tongue."[7] Mansfield spent hours in the English countryside living, through his imagination, the life of Richard as portrayed by Shakespeare. His approach to the role was consistent with his belief that the creative actor must first get the feeling of a role. The actor must grip the idea, the theme, the essence of the character before tackling the acting of the role.[8] His intent was to humanize the play and, in particular, the role of Richard by emphasizing psychology in characterization. "You may not like him," explained Mansfield, "but he is a 'being,' which is more than the ranting, raving sulky monstrosity you have been accustomed to was."[9]

The London engagement of *Richard III* opened on March 16, 1889, at the Globe Theatre, and the production received mixed, though generally positive reviews. According to the critic for *The Globe*, the reason for the production's success was three-fold: a version of the play which was actable within a reasonable amount of time, exciting spectacle, and a new and unique interpretation of Richard.[10] Mansfield's text,[11] which was published and sold in pamphlet form in the lobby of the theatre, was prefaced with a "Nota" in which Mansfield set forth the view he took of the play. Shakespeare, he said, in arranging the events of Gloster's life for dramatic treatment, distorted deeds and events; accordingly, it was difficult to follow history while following Shakespeare. "Yet," said Mansfield, "we surely may, while painting the life of Richard upon the stage, endeavor in some measure to make him appear as he really was, permitting his character to form with the march of events and his age to be somewhat measured by the date of his acts."[12] This concern for Richard's age was apparent in both the Mansfield text and in the Globe Theatre playbill (see Figure 1, 1a) which recorded the historical

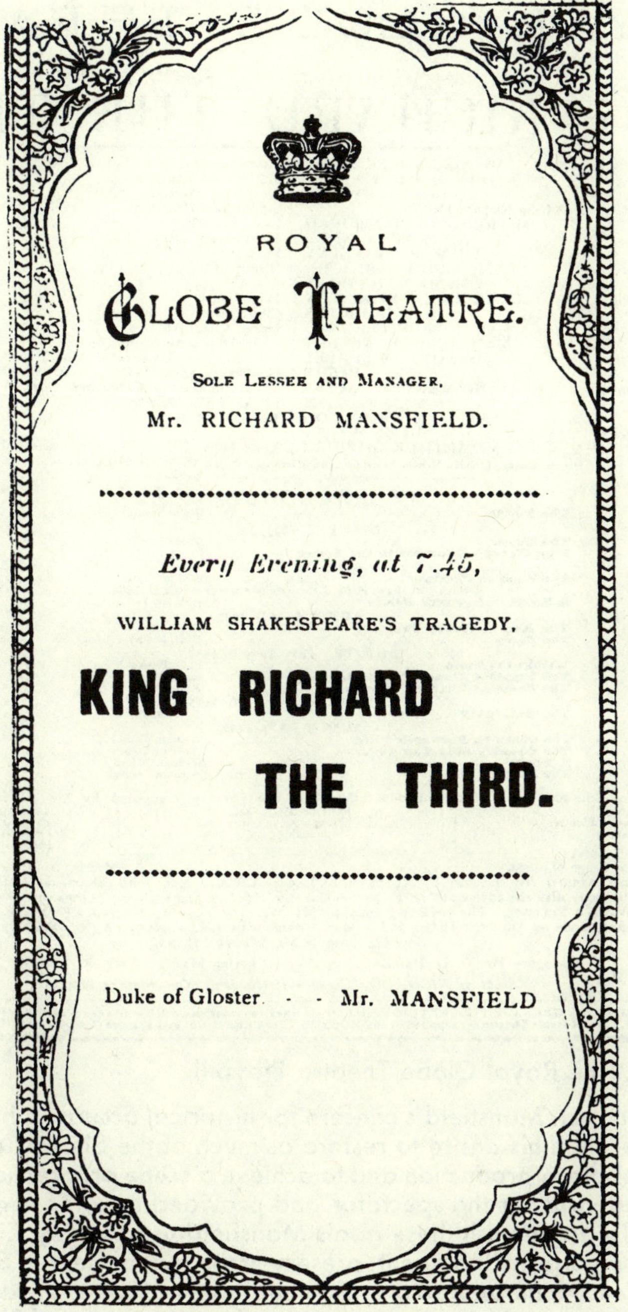
ROYAL

GLOBE THEATRE.

SOLE LESSEE AND MANAGER,

Mr. RICHARD MANSFIELD.

*Every Evening, at 7.45,*

WILLIAM SHAKESPEARE'S TRAGEDY,

KING RICHARD THE THIRD.

Duke of Gloster - - Mr. MANSFIELD

Figure 1. The Royal Globe Theatre Playbill.

# ROYAL GLOBE THEATRE.

Sole Lessee and Manager ... ... ... ... Mr. RICHARD MANSFIELD

EVERY EVENING, AT 7.45, WILLIAM SHAKESPEARE'S TRAGEDY.

# KING RICHARD THE THIRD.

| | | | |
|---|---|---|---|
| King Henry VI | Mr. ALLEN BEAUMONT | Sir James Tyrell | Mr. C. STEUART |
| Prince of Wales | Miss BESSIE HATTON | Sir Thomas Vaughan | Mr. EDGAR NORTON |
| Duke of York | Miss ISA BOWMAN | Sir Walter Herbert | Mr. C. SMILES |
| Duke of Gloster, afterwards King Richard III. | Mr. RICHARD MANSFIELD | Sir William Brandon | Mr. E. BROUGHTON |
| | | Earl of Pembroke | Mr. H. DRUCE |
| Duke of Buckingham | Mr. JAMES FERNANDEZ | Marquis of Dorset | Mr. M. BUIST |
| Duke of Norfolk | Mr. W. R. STAVELEY | Lord Lovell | Mr. L. DU BARRI |
| Earl of Richmond | Mr. LUIGI LABLACHE | Bishop of Ely | Mr. SYDNEY PRICE |
| Lord Stanley | Mr. D. H. HARKINS | Abbot | Mr. A. SIMS |
| Sir Richard Ratcliffe | Mr. REGINALD STOCKTON | Wyndham | Mr. F. VIVIAN |
| Earl of Oxford | Mr. J. BURROWS | Court Jester | Mr. F. W. KNIGHT |
| Lord Mayor of London | Mr. JOSEPH FRANKAU | Queen Elizabeth | Miss MARY RORKE |
| Sir James Blount | Mr. LEONARD CALVERT | Lady Attendants to the Queen | |
| Sir William Catesby | Mr. NORMAN FORBES | | Miss BURTON, Miss LANGTON, Miss OLLIFFE |
| Earl of Surrey | Mr. J. PARRY | Duchess of York | Miss CARLOTTA LECLERCQ |
| Sir Robert Brakenbury | Mr. MERVYN DALLAS | Lady Attendant to the Duchess | Mrs. WHITTIER CHANDOS |
| Berkeley | Mr. J. G. SLEE | Margaret Plantagenet | Miss E. ORFORD |
| Lord Hastings | Mr. W. H CROMPTON | Edward Plantagenet | Miss N. BOWMAN |
| Captain of the Guard | Mr. H. WYATT | AND | |
| Tressel | Mr. ARTHUR GILMORE | Lady Anne | Miss BEATRICE CAMERON |

*Priests, Monks, Acolytes, Men-at-Arms, Citizens, Merchants, Pages, Archers, Aldermen, Children, &c., &c.*

## *PROLOGUE.*

| | | | |
|---|---|---|---|
| | **The Tower** | Bruce Smith | *Three minutes' interval* |
| | **ACT I.—May, 1471.** | | |
| Scene I. | **The Tower** | Bruce Smith | |
| Scene II. | **King Henry's Chamber in the Tower** | Bruce Smith | *An interval of ten minutes* |
| | **ACT II.—May, 1471.** | | |
| Scene I. | **The Road to Chertsey** | William Telbin | *An interval of four minutes* |
| | Twelve years have elapsed, the date of events being **A.D. 1483.** | | |
| Scene II. | **A Room in Baynard Castle** | William Telbin | *An interval of ten minutes* |
| | **ACT III.—A.D. 1483.** | | |
| Scene I. | **The Hall in Crosby Palace** | E. G. Banks | |
| Scene II. | **The Same** | E. G. Banks | *An interval of ten minutes* |
| | **ACT IV., Part 1.—A.D. 1483.** | | |
| Scene I. | **Within the Tower** | E. G. Banks | *An interval of one minute* |
| Scene II. | **The Presence Chamber (morning)** | E. G. Banks | |
| Scene III. | **The Presence Chamber (evening)** | E. G. Banks | *An interval of ten minutes* |
| | **ACT IV., Part 2.—A.D. 1485.** | | |
| Scene I. | **The Sanctuary** | E. G. Banks | *An interval of ten minutes* |
| | **ACT V.—A.D. 1485.** | | |
| Scene I. | **The Camp on Bosworth Field** | William Telbin | *An interval of two minutes* |
| Scene II. | **The Country near Tamworth** | William Telbin | *An interval of one minute* |
| Scene III. | **A Glade** | William Telbin | |
| Scene IV. | **The Battle Field** | William Telbin | |

The Overture, Entr'actes, and all the Incidental Music to the Tragedy, composed by Mr. EDWARD GERMAN

| | | |
|---|---|---|
| Overture | Allegretto Grazioso | Andante Sostenuto |
| Intermezzo Funebre | Menuetto | Allegro Risoluto |
| Pastorale | Interlude | Prelude |
| | | Marcia Maestoso |

Stage Manager - - - - - - - - - - - - - Mr. E. B. NORMAN.

The Costumes, Armour, &c., designed by Mr. SEYMOUR LUCAS, A.R.A., F.S.A., with the assistance of Mr. F. WEEKES. The Military Archæology with the advice of Mr. EGERTON CASTLE, F.S.A. The Fighting Scenes with the advice of Mr. CASTLE and Mr. WALTER POLLOCK. The Scenery painted by Mr. WILLIAM TELBIN, Mr. BRUCE SMITH, Mr. E. G. BANKS. Costumes made by AUGUSTE ET CIE and S. MAY. Armour by J. L. KENNEDY & Co. Wigs by C. H. FOX. New Act Drop by Mr. WALTER HANN.

Manager—Mr. E. D. PRICE. Acting Manager—Mr. R. REDFORD.

*Books of RICHARD III. of the Attendants, One Shilling each.*

IMPERIAL GRENADE FIRE EXTINGUISHERS are fitted up throughout this Theatre as a provision against Fire. All ICES sold at this Theatre are supplied by the HORTON ICE CREAM Co., and Tea and Coffee by DAKIN & COMPY.

Figure 1a. The Royal Globe Theatre Playbill.

date of each act. Mansfield's concern for historical accuracy, however, was no stronger than his desire to restore as much of the Shakespearean verse as was feasible in production and to achieve a scene progression which was smooth and swift for the spectator and provided time for numerous scene changes. To accomplish these goals Mansfield used Colley Cibber's 1700 version as an organizing agent; preserved the five-act text of Shakespeare, much condensed; introduced only small portions of Cibber's text for purposes of transition or emotional effect; and introduced a portion of Shakespeare's *Henry VI, Parts 2 and 3* and a few lines from Shakespeare's *Henry IV, Parts*

*1 and 2, Henry V,* and *Richard II*. Following Cibber's 1700 version, Mansfield deleted the Clarence plot and omitted the characters of Clarence, Margaret and Edward IV.

Most of the negative London reviewers and some of the positive reviewers cited Mansfield's use of Cibber as a shortcoming; however, most reviewers approved Mansfield's hybridization of Shakespeare and Cibber. The critic for *The Stage* praised the clarity of Mansfield's version;[13] the critic for *The Tablet* appreciated the playable length of Mansfield's text and defended Mansfield's use of Cibber's scene progression by noting that Garrick, Kemble, and Charles Kean had also thought it an improvement for acting purposes.[14] It should be noted that the Cibber version of *Richard III* had held the stage in England and America for nearly 200 years, with only a few attempts at restoring Shakespeare during the nineteenth century. Henry Irving returned to Shakespeare's text in his 1877 production, but Irving cut the play's length by half. He reduced Margaret to one scene, her first, and cut her heavily afterwards; severely shortened the dream and murder of Clarence and the arrest of Hastings; and omitted the scene with the women before the Tower in Act IV. In actuality, then, Irving merely found a means other than the Cibber version to shorten the play. His cutting was not a good one; indeed, George Odell considered his version "almost unintelligible."[15] Edwin Booth employed William Winter's version of Shakespeare's play in his 1878 production, which took even greater liberties with the text than had Irving's version the year before. Winter cut thirteen of the thirty-seven characters, including the princes; produced a division of acts to bring into prominence the episodes connected with Clarence and Hastings; and reduced, shifted and rearranged many of the scenes to effect a text of approximately half the length of Shakespeare's. Neither Irving's nor Booth's version, then, was a complete return to Shakespeare, and Booth even reverted to the Cibber version in 1886 in his last production of *Richard III*.[16]

How totally Mansfield's intentions for staging were realized may be ascertained from reviewers' descriptions of the London premiere and subsequent American performances, and from George Becks' promptbook of Mansfield's production.[17] The performance began with an overture by Edward German. Indeed, German's music scored the entire play and included incidental music, *entr'actes, leitmotives* for the principal characters, and old English melodies to evoke a sense of period atmosphere.[18] The stage action began with the scene from *Henry VI, Part 3* in which Tressel delivers news of Prince Edward's death and orders come for Henry's confinement to the Tower. The Tower and drawbridge provided the setting (see Figure 2b), and green calcium lights created the "pale white light" of morning which Mansfield required.[19] There followed immediately a procession of Edward IV's Queen Elizabeth. Scored by triumphal music, the procession wound from downstage right, across the walkway, over the drawbridge, and through the gateway to the Tower. The critic for *The Star* described the action in some detail.

*Presently the role of the drum is heard, the warders form a cor-*

Figure 2. "The Wooing of Lady Anne". The following illustrations (2, 2a, b, c, d) are from a full page compilation of scenes from the Mansfield production in *The Illustrated Sporting and Dramatic News,* March 23, 1889. Photo courtesy Newspaper Library of the British Library.

> *don, pressing back the crowd with their bills, and a martial procession sweeps across the stage, heralds, men-at-arms, a mitred bishop, Benedictine monks in black and white. Then Edward IV's Queen Elizabeth . . . in stiff brocade and quaint 'butterfly' headgear . . . advancing slowly under a canopy. And now . . . the tail of the procession disappears under the portcullis, . . . .*[20]

There followed Gloster's opening monologue, and immediately thereafter a change of setting to "Henry's Chamber in the Tower."

An ink sketch of Henry's chamber (Figure 2d) and George Becks' promptbook ground plan reveal that the scenery and lighting gave form to Mansfield's mental images at Bournemouth. Red light spilled over the fireplace area, moonlight poured through the stained glass window above the oratory, and natural blue moonlight entered the stage through a window upstage of Henry's bed. The critic for the *Daily Chronicle* described this as a "grim setting" for Henry's murder by Gloster.[21]

Mansfield began his Act II with the wooing of Anne and placed it on a beautiful country road on the outskirts of London rather than in the traditional London street. The promptbook ground plan and an ink sketch (Figure 2) reveal how well Mansfield achieved on stage his imagined vision. A three-dimensional tree, realistic in detail, occupied center stage, a grassy mound occupied downstage right, and walls of houses covered with ivy bounded the stage right and up left. A fence completed the scenic encirclement downstage left. The remainder of Act II, presenting the two children of Clarence and the lamentation for Clarence and Edward IV, was not cited by London and American critics. But Mansfield's Act III (presenting the episode of the boy princes, the condemnation of Hastings, and the plot with Buckingham to gain the crown) which took place in "The Hall in Crosby Palace," was cited by almost all the critics as one of the most splendid interiors in the production. An ink sketch (Figure 2c) of the stage left side of this setting exhibits wood beaming, a practical, bannistered landing, a practical staircase, and a beamed ceiling. The promptbook provides a ground plan for scene one, revealing the use of side lighting through the arches and stained glass windows.

Mansfield's IV, Part 1, scene one presented the capture of the princes, and this setting was described by the critic for *The Stage* as "another fine bit of stage masonry, in which the stonework stands out as if in reality it existed."[22] Part 1, scene two presented the temptations of Buckingham and Tyrrel. The setting, "The Presence Chamber," was another splendid interior which, according to the ground plan, incorporated a large arched entrance stage right, raised several feet, with four or five steps down to the stage floor. The throne, displaying a white rose emblem, sat center stage. The lighting was quite bright to indicate morning, and two stained glass windows appeared high in the wall up stage left. Scene three, in which Richard learns of the princes' murder, was set in the same chamber. A lighting change, however, created the effect of an evening scene and caused the light through stained glass windows to come into prominence.

Figure 2a. "The Sanctuary".

Waiting to hear the news of the deaths of the princes, Mansfield was alone in the throne room. Filled with a sense of security and gratified ambition, he mounted the throne chair and sat in it with every evidence of satisfaction. As he did so, red light streamed through stained glass windows and fell with the color of blood upon his face and hands. The music, which was peculiar to the princes, and which had been heard whenever they had appeared, a sweet, low, touching strain, was played, and the audience at once felt that Richard was thinking of the murdered innocents and that the red light suggested to him nothing but blood.[23] Terror-stricken, he slid from the throne and sat brooding at its foot. Here is an excellent example of Mansfield's use of lighting and music to evoke a particularly macabre atmosphere.

The critic for *The Stage* described Richard's camp in Act V as "a most imposing stage picture."[24] According to the promptbook, at the rear of the setting was a drop of Richard's camp with painted tents and watchfires. A low hedgerow ran across backstage at the foot of the drop, and forest wings appeared stage right. Richard's tent was placed down left, a table containing a helmet and maps was right of the tent, and a fire was right of the table. Richard's bed was placed inside the tent and was visible to the audience. From the opening of the scene until the nightmare sequence, drum beats sounded in the distance. As Mansfield lay down to sleep, the drums and lights faded, and a gray gauze dropped into position at the hedgerow line. Dull white light was then projected onto the gray-clad ghosts, who appeared

Figure 2b. "The Tower".

behind the gauze. Again, Mansfield took great pains to create mood — in this instance, the mood of doom.

The final setting, "The Battlefield," revealed "realistically painted dead bodies" on a mound upstage left and under a tree downstage right; and a practical bridge appeared upstage right.[25] This uncluttered setting provided space for Mansfield's innovative staging of the final catastrophe on Bosworth Field. Maintaining his concern for historical accuracy, the actor employed the large, heavy swords and shields of the Plantagenet era rather than fencing instruments. The sounds of battle — swords clashing and soldiers screaming — were heard throughout the battle, and the play ended with cheers for the new King Henry VII.

Almost all the London reviewers were ecstatic in their praise of Mansfield's staging. Many labeled it superior to all previous productions of the play in London, specifically to Charles Kean's revival some thirty-five years earlier and to the more recent revivals of Irving and Bateman.[26] The staging of Irving's 1877 production, while beautiful, was not extravagant. Indeed, in a speech to the Garrick Club, Irving cited that production as an instance where success was not achieved through splendid settings.[27] Only ten sets were employed; these included three front scenes and two scenes which were probably drops in the third or fourth grooves. One of the interior box sets was made to serve as two rooms in the palace by the insertion of a fireplace in a doorway. And whenever two full stage sets were used in the same act, Irving interposed a carpenter's scene.[28] Mansfield's 1889 production employed eleven sets, six exteriors and five interiors, and of these only the two scenes depicting Richmond's preparations for battle incorporated drops alone. The interior scenes were consistently praised for their solid and architectural appearance; and most of the exterior scenes were made highly realistic by the inclusion of trees, walls of houses, fences, and shrubbery (the

2c. "Crosby Hall" and the Princes.

Figure 2d. "The Duke of Gloucester, Queen Elizabeth, and Richmond". "The Oratory".

Road to Chertsey), by building facades (the street outside the Sanctuary in Act IV), or by other architectural features (the Tower in the opening scene, the bridge on the battlefield). The twelve years that passed between Irving's and Mansfield's productions brought considerable advances in the "Theatre of Illusion." Accordingly, a more meaningful comparison might be made between Mansfield's 1889 production and Irving's productions of *Faust* in 1885 and *Henry VIII* in 1892.

Beginning with Irving's *Romeo and Juliet* in 1882, five years after he premiered *Richard III*, the Lyceum productions became increasingly correct and spectacular under the influence of scholarly painters engaged to design sets and costumes. Alan Hughes suggests that the climax came with *Henry VIII* (1892) with costumes designed by Seymour Lucas, the artist who supervised costumes and armor for Mansfield's *Richard III*. William Telbin, who painted several settings for Mansfield's production, served as one of the primary scenic artists on Irving's *Faust*. And Telbin's and Hawes Craven's designs for *Faust* were praised for many of the features possessed by Mansfield's settings for *Richard III*: archaeological accuracy, technical realism of detail, and period flavor.[29] Faust's study, for example, was a high, narrow Gothic chamber containing a massive reading desk heaped with volumes of manuscripts. Above the desk the dried carcass of an alligator hung from the ceiling, and shelves of books covered the walls. The whole setting evoked "the very spirit of musty Gothicism," and was "a thoroughly authentic and atmospheric period set."[30] A low-burning lamp sat on the desk, and pale silver moonlight fell softly across the floor and touched the table near which Faust sat.[31] The mood generated by the atmospheric setting and lighting are reminiscent of Mansfield's setting for Henry VI's chamber in the Tower. Finally, Irving maintained an orchestra which played overtures and *entr'actes* composed by resident or guest composers. Incidental music was also frequently employed to prepare moods and underlie emotions, although this was more often the case in Irving's productions of melodrama than in his stagings of Shakespeare.[32] While Mansfield's use of lighting and music was exceptionally artistic in its choice of materials and in its execution, then, it was merely in keeping with the developing "Theatre of Illusion." But Mansfield's production was, up to its time, the most elaborate rendering of Shakespeare's play ever seen on the London stage.

Mansfield claimed never to have seen a production of *Richard III*; accordingly, his interpretation of Gloster was free from any preconception. Despite his research of the historical figure and despite his concern for dating the play's events, however, Mansfield's rendering of Gloster was not a radical departure from that of Edwin Booth or Henry Irving. Indeed, William Winter asserted that Mansfield's portrayal followed the "Kean and Booth tradition of the past."[33] Like Booth and Irving, Mansfield contrasted the cold malignity and sardonic ease of the murdering Gloster in the early acts with the tormented and remorseful King in Act V, and he based his costumes and make-up on historical portraits. Except in a few instances, he chose Shakespeare's more subtle characterization over the melodramatic villain who struts through Colley Cibber's version. In his "new" interpretation, Mansfield toned the grotesque nature of the character, as did Booth and Irving, but, more than his predecessors, he concentrated on Richard's intellect and motives for action. In a few unfortunate instances Mansfield injured his naturalistic portrayal by playing too broadly, and some critics were quick to complain.

Mansfield's biographers, William Winter and Paul Wilstach, maintained that the actor's interpretation of Richard and his stage business remained consistent throughout the first London and American engagements and in the revivals of 1896-97 and 1905. Accordingly, reviews of Mansfield's acting in several performances may be combined to provide as full a description as possible. According to William Winter, Mansfield's portrayal had not "even the faintest reminiscence of the ranting, mouthing, flannel-jawed king of clubs who has so generally strutted and bellowed as Shakespeare's Gloster."[34] The reviewer for the *New York Times* stated that Mansfield's Richard was "neither tigerish nor malignant. He was quiet, ruthless and entirely human."[35] Another New York critic commended Mansfield for bringing psychological validity and credibility to the story. Mansfield, he said, was the first of all actors to make Richard "natural and possible."[36] And the critic for the London *Stage* stated that Mansfield made Richard "a plotting, scheming man, who appears from the opening of the play to be overshadowed by some awful fate."[37]

Mansfield's interpretation of Richard was evident from his first speech, "now is the winter of our discontent," which he spoke quietly, preserving the verse and meter of the lines. His decision to subdue Richard's physical deformities, to emphasize his youth, and to play the opening soliloquy for simplicity and subtlety provided a strong naturalistic base from which the character could grow in emotional power and psychological torment. Interestingly, Mansfield omitted the opening monologue in some American performances. Presumably his intent was to remove altogether the early references to Richard's deformity and pursuit of evil.

In his second scene, Mansfield murdered Henry cooly and unconcernedly. Reviewing the scene as played in a New York revival of 1905, the critic for *The Sun* described Mansfield's attitude as "youthfully lighthearted, cynical — even casual. He loafs with ungainly grace about the stage, cooly calculating the exquisite moment in which to run the aged king through . . . "[38] John Ranken Towse's description of the scene as played in another New York performance is quite evocative.

> *His entrance into King Henry's chamber in the tower, his studied pause upon the threshold, his warming of his hands at the fire, the careful arrangement of his pose against the wall at the head of the King's bed, his deliberate drawing of his sword, and the testing of the tip exhibited a calculated mechanism in which there was no quiver of life or emotion. He passed his sword through the body of his victim with the nonchalance of a poulterer skewering a fowl, and wiped his sword upon the curtain with the same passionless indifference.*[39]

Richard's first murder on stage, as performed by Mansfield, maintained the realistic presentation of a character motivated by ambition and operating in a period in which violence was a way of life.[40]

In the wooing of Anne, Mansfield was described by Paul Wilstach as "a mad-cap of such cheerful irony that Lady Anne found him more irresistible than impossible. . . . "[41] Charlotte Porter, however, suggested that Mansfield was much too obvious in this scene. The actor, she said, "makes the mistake . . . of showing the audience that he is calculating his words and actions, and watching too narrowly the progress of their effect upon his dupe.

He makes us feel that Anne herself should have been undeceived by such posturing."[42]

Porter also complained that Mansfield was over-theatrical in the Mayor and citizens scene. When Richard met the Mayor and citizens of London, he was flipping through the pages of a prayerbook, posing as a pious man. Convinced of his good intentions the Mayor and citizens requested he accept the crown. After their exit, Richard discovered he had been holding the prayerbook upside down. He turned the book over with a sarcastic smile, then flung it triumphantly over his shoulder.[43] According to the promptbook, he then crossed to the throne and rose to his full height with his hands on the arms. The curtain fell on Mansfield in this position, with a look on his face which indicated, "We got there!" Porter felt the Mayor and citizens would have to be blind not to have noted the very elaborate turning of the pages of the upside down prayerbook.[44] Mansfield's severest critic, J. Ranken Towse, also asserted that the actor overplayed the character's hypocrisy; in addition Towse claimed that Mansfield emphasized the character's deformity and tottered around and limped in a manner inconsistent with the historical figure he meant to portray.[45] From photographs of Mansfield in costume, it is apparent that the actor made the slight deformity more pronounced as the character grew older, although when dressed in armor in Act V, he showed no evidence of a hump at all (see Mansfield in costume, Figures 3 through 7). A more pronounced deformity as the play progressed is not contradictory to Mansfield's psychological portrayal. Richard's physical deformity merely increased somewhat as the character aged. But, for a few critics Mansfield played some moments too broadly and out of character with his historical conception of Richard. The scene with the prayerbook was also one of the few times Mansfield resorted to traditional business for Gloster. Cibber had also flung the prayerbook into the air on the Mayor's exit.[46]

Most critics agreed that Acts IV and V were the highlight of Mansfield's acting. In Act IV, said the critic for *The Star,* Mansfield "reaches and preserves the true tragic pitch and of itself his playing at this critical juncture will, I think, establish beyond cavil his right to rank, and to rank high, among Shakespearean actors."[47] Paul Wilstach offered the most definitive and concise statement concerning Mansfield's acting of these scenes. "It was ever in scenes displaying the force of avenging conscience that Mansfield's imagination triumphed over his material and over the spectator most completely."[48] Thus, the moment described earlier, when Mansfield slid to the foot of the throne with red light from stained glass windows streaming onto his person, was an intense moment for the audience. This was the first revelation of Richard's inner struggle with his own conscience, and, according to William Winter, Mansfield was the first actor to reveal the King's conscience this early in the play. Edwin Booth showed the first signs of Richard's dread and vacillation after the queen-mother spoke her curse late in Act IV;[49] Henry Irving waited as late as the tent scene in Act V.[50]

One of the most impressive aspects of Mansfield's acting in Act V was the way in which he caused the character to age as a result of time passage

Figure 3. Mansfield and Beatrice Cameron, The Wooing of Anne, II i. From Winter, *Richard Mansfield,* 1:122.

and evil deeds. William Winter described how Mansfield marked the difference the years had made in Richard.

> *The gay, blithe, jaunty, cynical demeanor of the Duke of Gloster thus, slowly, but with a fine force of contrast, lapses into the fevered, restless, watchful, suspicious, arrogant, and defiant demeanor of the haunted desperate King. . . . The nervous system becomes enfeebled, almost shattered; the frame is emaciated; the eyes are cavernous; the voice has become harsh and strident; the body, except for an occasional movement of stealthy, vigilant, self-enforced calm, or of the lethargy of abject fatigue, moves continually. . . .*[51]

In his 1877 production Henry Irving also contrasted the energetic Richard of the early scenes with the careworn tyrant of the final act. But Irving did not date the play's events or mark the character's aging with make-up. His Richard was young throughout the play, although he seemed prematurely old and weary at the play's end.[52] In his 1896 revival, Richard was old, or at least middle-aged, from the start.[53]

In Act V Mansfield walked toward his tent to sleep, plagued by a tormented conscience, when suddenly he saw a shadow. Imagining it to be someone, he whirled, drew his sword, and duelled desperately with the phantom until, in his imagination, he had won. He then lay down to sleep. This was an entirely new approach to the moment. Edmund Kean had stopped before entering his tent to sketch on the ground a plan for the morrow's battle. Kean had completed his plan in triumph and then walked into his tent with confidence.[54] And Irving had held the audience spellbound through two or three silent minutes while he studied maps, warmed his hands at the brazier, and gazed out moodily into the night.[55] But Mansfield's business evoked a greater degree of self doubt and a stronger sense that the character's fears were bringing on hallucinations. Such business also foreshadowed the appearance of the ghosts which followed.

Mansfield's handling of Richard's awaking from the nightmare was masterful. Even Catesby, at first, to the rudely awakened King was another avenging spirit. Rapidly and repeatedly, in terror, Mansfield made the sign of the cross and finally reached out and touched Catesby to make sure that he was flesh and blood. Satisfied, he fell exhausted upon Catesby's breast. According to one writer, the effect of this new business, "so appropriate to the situation," was "electrical."[56] This business is identical to Mansfield's imagined playing of the scene recorded in his article. Those scenes the actor imagined in such detail while at Bournemouth became "electrical" moments on stage. Mansfield demonstrated a freshness of invention in his approach to a play with tired, old, traditional by-play. His business was new-born, full of surprise, not burdened with cliché. While Kean had "started" at Catesby's entrance, and Kemble had actually fallen into Catesby's arms,[57] Mansfield was the first to fully explore this moment in terms of the character's psychology. Mansfield emphasized the character's delirium, as though the

Figure 4. Mansfield as Glo'ster, Act III. From Winter, *Richard Mansfield,* 2:48.

phantoms had thrown him into a frenzy of remorse and hysterical fear. According to William Winter, in this scene, "The 'Jesu have mercy' came forth in a shriek of agony, and the entire speech was delivered in one prolonged torrent of fluent frenzy, and with a glorious volume of voice the like of which has seldom been heard." Mansfield rose "to the full height of physical, spiritual, and vocal expression . . . " and yet preserved "such complete control of all the faculties as to impart conviction of power still held in reserve. . . . A more satisfying exhibiton of the union of intellectual and physical powers has seldom if ever been seen upon the stage."[58]

During the final struggle Mansfield, dressed in armor (Figure 7), hacked a lane through his foes with his sword, then single handedly guarded a bridge against a host of the enemy until at length he was beaten back and overborn by sheer weight of numbers. When he reappeared alone upon another part of the field and was urged by Catesby to fly, he stood for a moment like the incarnation of despair, then determined to "stand the hazard of the die." He singled out "the sixth Richmond," and fought again with "the fury of a fiend."[59] One writer found the final struggle between Richard and Richmond at the play's conclusion "intensely exciting."

> *With all their strength Richard and Richmond slash each other with their swords. . . . Finally the weakened King staggers, his blows lose their force, he flings away his shield that he may grasp his sword with both hands and again renew the attack. Richmond stabs him in a vital part, and he staggers away only to return, weaponless, to the attack, and filled with the spirit of murder, he strikes the victorious Richmond with his mailed fist. Struck down again, his face terrible with the expression of mingled hate and despair, he dies, grasping at the air as if he still saw within his reach some coveted prize. . . . Throughout the whole of the conflict the sounds of the raging battle are heard. The drums beat, the trumpets sound, the cries of the wounded and the dying pierce the air, and the clanking of the armors and the clash of steel make the harsh music of conflict, and the scene is brilliant with the waving banners and the various devices and colors which mark the rank and estate of the personages engaged.*[60]

According to this critic, the scene aroused the audience to the wildest enthusiasm, and the curtain fell amid the plaudits of the spectators.

Clearly Mansfield was more successful in creating Richard's historical era on stage than he was in rendering a historical character. His interpretation, which he believed to be new, was, in fact, similar to that of Henry Irving and Edwin Booth. In the last quarter of the nineteenth century intelligent actors sought to humanize a Shakespearean character, even a villain such as Gloster. Mansfield followed this trend, and perhaps even made strides by acting Gloster with more naturalism than had his predecessors.

Mansfield's *Richard III* was the first brave venture of an ambitious, aesthetically high principled, eventually famous star. Inspired by Mansfield's New York premiere in 1889, William Winter wrote that the actor's continued

Figure 5. Mansfield as Glo'ster, Act III. From Winter, *Richard Mansfield*, 2:56.

success meant the advancement of the American theatre. "At no time," he said, "has a public duty been more clearly obvious than is at this moment the duty of the intellectual portion of this community — the men and women who really know anything about the art of acting and really value and esteem it — to sustain this intrepid actor in the noble enterprise upon which he has embarked."[61] Such enthusiasm from such a discerning critic could only have been stimulated by a production of the highest artistic merit. With *Richard III* Mansfield threw off the weeds of a matinee idol and accepted the responsibilities of a serious theatre artist.

## NOTES

[1]William Winter, *The Life and Art of Richard Mansfield,* 2 vols. (New York: Moffat, Yard & Co., 1910), 1:83.

[2]Richard Mansfield, "The Story of a Production," *Harper's Weekly,* May 24, 1890, p. 408.

[3]"Story of a Production," p. 408.

[4]"Story of a Production," p. 408.

[5]Paul Wilstach, *Richard Mansfield: The Man and the Actor* (New York: C. Scribner & Sons, 1908), p. 180.

[6]"Story of a Production," p. 408.

[7]"Story of a Production," p. 408.

[8]James O'Donnell Bennet, "Richard Mansfield," (*Munsey's Magazine,* March 1907), p. 776.

[9]"Story of a Production," p. 408.

[10]*The Globe* (London), 18 March 1889, p. 7.

[11]William Shakespeare, *King Richard the Third,* ed. Richard Mansfield (London: Partridge & Cooper, 1889).

[12]Wilstach, *Man and the Actor,* pp. 178-179.

[13]*The Stage* (London), 22 March 1889, p. 10.

[14]*The Tablet* (London), 23 March 1889, p. 443.

[15]George C. D. Odell, *Shakespeare from Betterton to Irving,* 2 vols. (New York: Charles Scribner's Sons, 1920), 2:310.

[16]Alice I. Perry Wood, *The Stage History of Shakespeare's King Richard the Third* (New York: Columbia University Press, 1909), p. 159.

[17]George Becks, ed. *King Richard the Third as Arranged for Production at the Globe Theatre March 16, 1889.* Promptbook for the Mansfield Production, Lincoln Center Theatre Collection, New York City.

[18]See *The Stage* (London), 22 March 1889, p. 10 and *New York Times,* December 17, 1889, p. 4 for more detailed comments on German's score.

[19]Becks.

[20]*The Star* (London), 18 March 1889, p. 2.

[21]*Daily Chronicle* (London), 18 March 1889, p. 5.

[22]*The Stage* (London), 22 March 1889, p. 10.

[23]*Boston Herald,* 22 October 1889, p. 5.

[24]*The Stage* (London), 22 March 1889, p. 10.

[25]*The Stage* (London), 22 March 1889, p. 10.

[26]Unidentified press clipping, Victoria and Albert Museum, London.

[27]Wood, p. 130.

[28]Alan Hughes, *Henry Irving, Shakespearean* (London: Cambridge University Press, 1981), p. 156.

[29]Michael R. Booth, *Victorian Spectacular Theatre, 1850-1910* (London: Routledge & Kegan Paul, 1981), pp. 98-99.

Figure 6. Mansfield as Glo'ster, Act IV. From Winter, *Richard Mansfield,* 2:60.

[30]Booth, p. 103.

[31]Booth, p. 103.

[32]Hughes, pp. 17-18.

[33]William Winter, *Life and Art of Edwin Booth* (Boston: Joseph Knight Company, 1893), p. 319.

[34]Winter, *Life and Art of Richard Mansfield*, 2:53.

[35]*New York Times*, 17 December 1889, p. 4.

[36]*Spirit of the Times* (New York), 21 December 1889, p. 8.

[37]*The Stage* (London), 22 March 1889, p. 10.

[38]*New York Sun*, 22 March 1905, p. 7.

[39]John R. Towse, *Sixty Years in the Theatre: An Old Critic's Memories* (New York: Funk and Wagnalls Co., 1916), p. 326.

[40]Mansfield's purpose in portraying this murder from Shakespeare's *Henry VI, Part 3* rather than the murder of Clarence from Shakespeare's *Richard III* was probably three-fold: (1) the murder of Henry provided a direct, dramatic encounter between Gloster and his victim and offered the star an effective early moment on stage; (2) it provided a sense of progression from the events of the earlier chronicle play to the events of *Richard III*, a play which essentially continues the story of the War of the Roses; and (3) it removed a long scene in which Gloster is not a character (Clarence's dream and murder), shortened the play's running time, and emphasized the star role.

[41]Wilstach, *Man and the Actor*, p. 183.

[42]Charlotte Porter, "The Stage," *Poet-Lore*, Vol. II (1890), pp. 31-32.

[43]Clayton Hamilton, *Seen on Stage* (New York: H. Holt & Co., 1914), p. 47.

[44]Porter, p. 32.

[45]J. Ranken Towse, *Evening Post* (New York), 17 December 1889, p. 9.

[46]Arthur Colby Sprague, *Shakespeare and the Actors*(Cambridge, Mass.: Harvard University Press, 1944), p. 150.

[47]*The Star* (London), 18 March 1889. p. 2.

[48]Wilstach, *Man and the Actor*, p. 183.

[49]Winter, *Life and Art of Richard Mansfield*, 2:52.

[50]Hughes, p. 155.

[51]William Winter, *New York Daily Tribune*, 31 March 1906, p. 7.

[52]Hughes, p. 155.

[53]Hughes, p. 152.

[54]Sprague, p. 102.

[55]Hughes, p. 155.

[56]*Boston Herald*, 22 October 1889, p. 5.

[57]Sprague, p. 105.

[58]Winter, *Life and Art of Richard Mansfield*, 2:61.

[59]*The Tablet* (London), 23 March 1889, pp. 443-45.

[60]*Boston Herald*, 22 October 1889, p. 5.

[61]William Winter, *New York Daily Tribune*, 17 December 1889, p. 6.

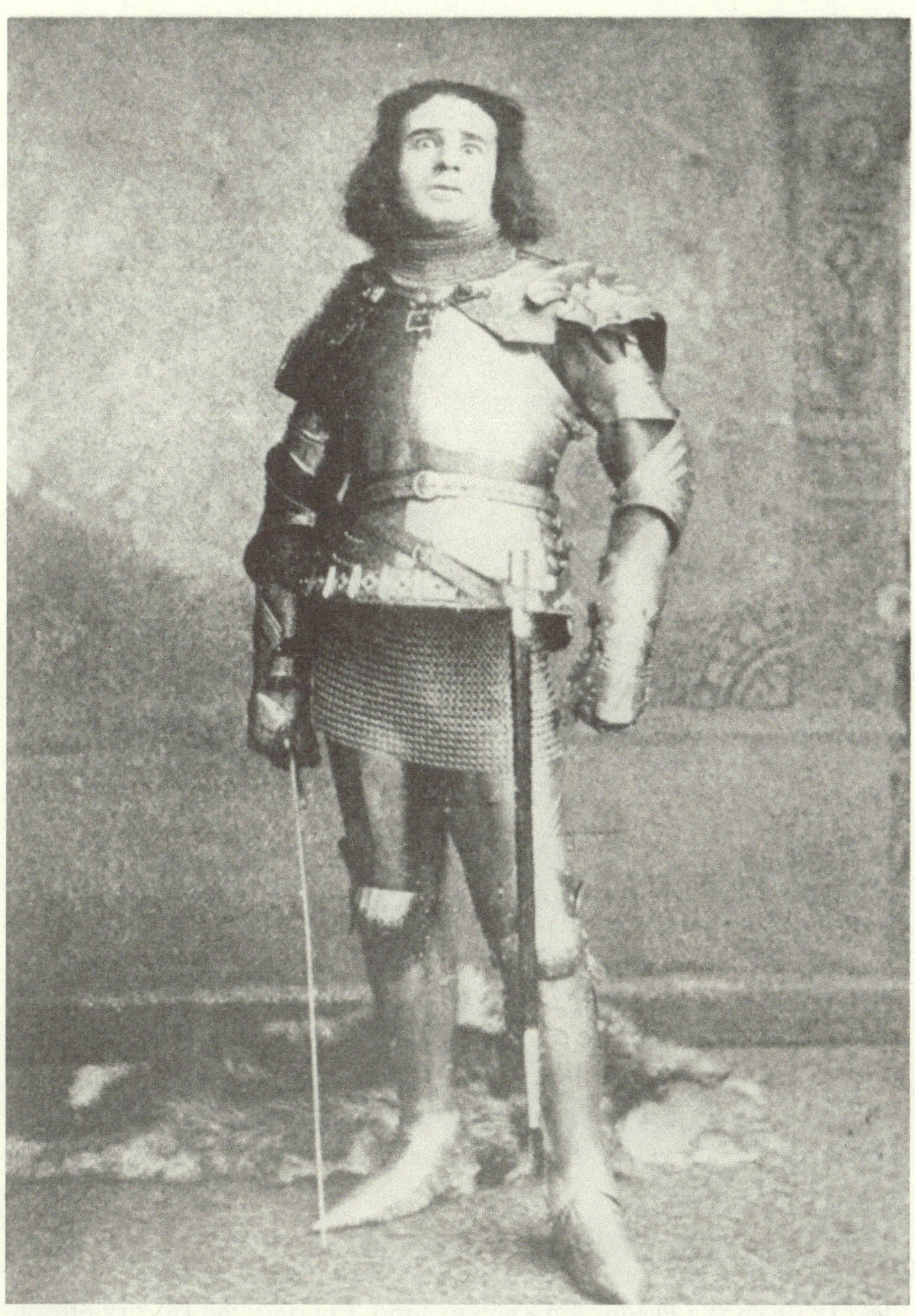

Figure 7. Mansfield as King Richard, Act V. From Winter, *Richard Mansfield,* 1:80.

The FTP Chicago *Othello*. Ian Keith as Iago. Courtesy the Library of Congress Federal Theatre Project Collection, at George Mason University Libraries, Fairfax, Virginia.

# The Shakespeare Productions of the Federal Theatre Project

STEPHEN M. VALLILLO

A renewed interest in the Federal Theatre Project recently has focused on the Project's network of regional theatres, its political controversies, and its innovative productions. When the Federal Theatre is mentioned, many people immediately think of the Living Newspaper productions or Orson Welles' "voodoo" *Macbeth*. This famous production was, however, only one of a number of Federal Theatre productions of the plays of Shakespeare. Together the Shakespeare productions illustrate the Federal Theatre's approach to performance. The productions did not follow the traditions of the past and the Federal Theatre's actors did not perform in the lyrical acting style of earlier Shakespeare productions, instead they took a more natural, if less poetic, approach. The productions were not chained to heavy, illusionistic scenery; they followed the new trends toward simplified sets. And startling new interpretations were presented, which often reflected the political climate.

Hallie Flanagan, the Project's national director, wrote in her book *Arena* that the Federal Theatre "was committed to the belief that a people's theatre could be occupied in no better way than by production of the classics."[1] Following this commitment the Federal Theatre produced Shakespeare, at least thirty-one productions in one form or another, from tabloids and marionette shows to full productions. Out of 830 major titles and a total of approximately 1,200 productions, the Shakespeare productions were a small but significant segment of the Federal Theatre.[2] Of twenty-eight full productions (as opposed to tabloid presentations combining several shows), eleven were tragedies and seventeen were comedies.

The productions of the tragedies emphasized both melodramatic spectacle and political overtones. With the exception of *Othello* and *Hamlet* in Chicago where the star, Ian Keith, was emulating Edwin Booth and a localized *Romeo and Juliet* in New Orleans, the only tragedies performed were plays about dictators or tyrants: *Macbeth*, which had five separate productions, *Coriolanus*, and *Julius Caesar*. The productions of *Julius Caesar* and *Coriolanus* left no doubt that the directors were attempting to draw parallels with the world situation of the time. *Julius Caesar's* Romans were dressed in Fascist blackshirts, and *Coriolanus* was described by the producers as Shakespeare's "timely play."[3] The *Macbeth* productions emphasized both the spectacle and melodrama more than the tragedy.

*Twelfth Night, The Taming of the Shrew* and *The Merry Wives of Windsor* were the most frequently performed comedies. These comedies had good

Stephen M. Vallillo is a Ph.D. candidate at New York University and a professional stage manager.

The FTP Chicago *Othello*. The city of Cyprus. Set design sketch by Clive Richabaugh. Courtesy the Library of Congress Federal Theatre Project Collection, at George Mason University Libraries, Fairfax, Virginia.

character roles for the many vaudeville and burlesque performers in the Federal Theatre casts. The comedies, with good character parts and funny, farcical situations, and the mysterious and spectacular tragedies, with the contemporary political commentaries, were probably welcome fare to the Depression audiences of the Federal Theatre.

Critics of the Project often questioned the ability of its actors. They believed that the actors were out of work because they were not good enough to get jobs. According to reviews and contemporary accounts, however, the performances were usually adequate, and often very good.

The type of performer used in the Shakespeare productions occasionally created problems. Older actors, with little or no training or experience in the classics, and ex-vaudevillians often constituted a large portion of the Federal Theatre casts. These actors frequently had difficulty with the verse and the style of the productions. John Grover, the director of *The Taming of the Shrew* in San Francisco in March 1936, complained about this in his report for the production bulletin:

> *. . . there were many factors which presented problems, mainly the actors themselves. Only two had played a line of Shakespeare before. . . . The older stock actors objected to the style, the idea, to the type of makeup required and the costumes as designed.*

The FTP Chicago *Othello*. The council chambers. Set design sketch by Clive Richabaugh. Courtesy the Library of Congress Federal Theatre Project Collection, at George Mason University Libraries, Fairfax, Virginia.

> *The hardest task was to make them think in terms of character relationships instead of actors and lines.*
>
> *Possibly the most difficult problem was combating an innate fear or downright dislike of anything remotely resembling verse. It was amazing to find trained actors with faulty speech and faulty memories coupled with a complete lack of imagination.*[4]

The Federal Theatre actors performing Shakespeare had a tendency to ignore, or at least downplay, the verse, emphasizing instead the emotion or action in a situation. In *Arena*, Hallie Flanagan tells of the first readthrough of *Julius Caesar* by the Delaware company. No one in the cast, which director Robert Schnitzer remembers as "not at all a distinguished group of performers," had ever read Shakespeare. But Schnitzer felt "the freshness of their readings gave new vigor to the play," and consequently led to his modern dress production.[5]

Some critics liked the tendency to emphasize action rather than poetry, but other critics did not find this approach appealing. One good example is the series of plays presented in Chicago during the spring and summer of 1939. The Chicago Federal Theatre chose to present a repertory of three plays, designed to star Ian Keith, an actor on the Project, who would also direct. Keith had been active on the American stage and screen since 1917,

The FTP Chicago *Hamlet*. The Ghost scene with Ian Keith as Hamlet. Courtesy the Library of Congress Federal Theatre Project Collection, at George Mason University Libraries, Fairfax, Virginia.

The FTP Los Angeles *The Merry Wives of Windsor*. Set design by Frederick Stover. Courtesy the Library of Congress Federal Theatre Project Collection, at George Mason University Libraries, Fairfax, Virginia.

and had extensive Shakespearean experience. He had also been married to Blanche Yurka.[6]

For Keith this was his opportunity to emulate and, supposedly follow in Edwin Booth's footsteps. He carefully chose *Othello, Hamlet* and *As You Like It*. In the first production, he played Iago the first week and Othello the next, following Booth's precedent. The acting version for *Hamlet*, which Keith adapted himself, closely followed Booth's.[7]

The critics generally liked Keith's performance in *Othello*, and felt that it far outdistanced the talent of the supporting cast. His approach to the poetry was especially praised in most reviews. The *Daily News* noted that "Mr. Keith sang the music without losing its meaning. . . . Give him an Iago and a Desdemona and he would give you a first rate Othello."[8]

For one critic, "What these actors lack in capacity to sing Shakespearean music they make up in naturalness, intensity of purpose and clarity of performance." But Ashton Stevens in the *Chicago American* felt Keith's performance showed "that most of the rest of the Federal Theatre troupers, many of them valuable in parts within their depth, would do well by themselves and the town to let William Shakespeare alone."[9]

Keith's *Hamlet* was in much the same vein. His version concentrated the chief soliloquies in one scene with only short breaks between them. Again the reviews generally praised his characterization and style, while recogniz-

The FTP San Francisco *The Taming of the Shrew*. Act II, scene i. Courtesy the Library of Congress Federal Theatre Project Collection, at George Mason University Libraries, Fairfax, Virginia.

ing that it overshadowed the rest of the company and bemoaning the lack of an adequate supporting cast. The *Daily Times* found that the "diction of many of the minor players often makes it difficult to hear the lines at the Keith delivery speed."[10]

After *Hamlet*, Ian Keith left the Project to work in Australia and Russell Spindler then directed the Chicago company's *As You Like It* as a " 'boy meets girl' story of an earlier era." The reviews reveal a much different style of interpretation than the previous productions with Ian Keith. The Chicago *Daily Tribune* pinpointed the difference. "Russell Spindler's direction is marked by a freedom from the sententiousness and the love of an older, bombastic style which were part of Ian Keith's whole concept of Shakespearean tradition."[11]

The Chicago series of plays also illustrates the Federal Theatre's approach to stage scenery. In principle, Hallie Flanagan, the national director, always advocated simplified stage settings and the increased use of lighting. For the Federal Theatre, where the funds were mandated largely for labor costs, this approach was almost a necessity.[12]

Most of the Project's productions used either one unit setting for the entire show, or a basic set to which elements were added and subtracted to

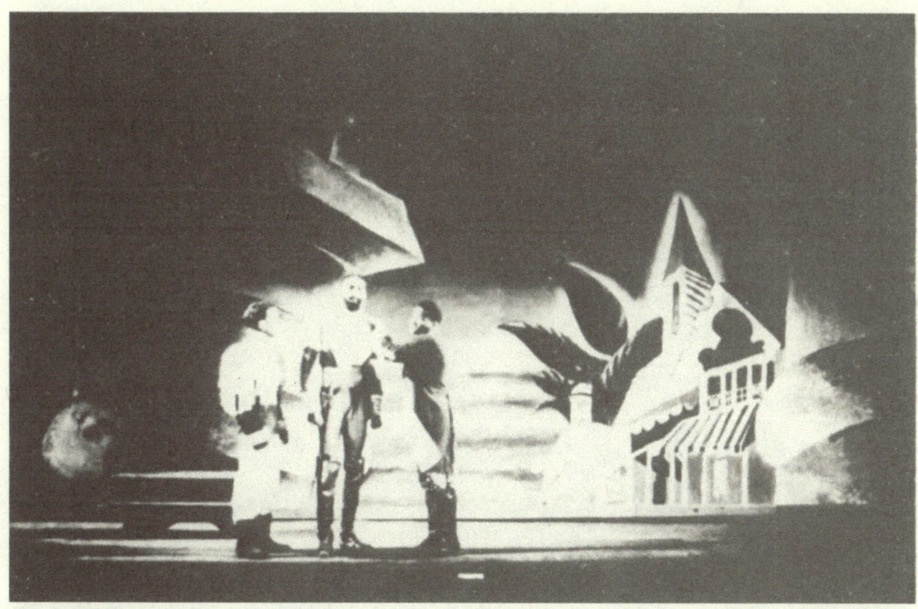

The FTP 1936 New York *Macbeth*. Maurice Ellis as Macduff learning of the death of his family. Courtesy the Billy Rose Theatre Collection, the New York Public Library at Lincoln Center, the Astor, Lenox and Tilden Foundations.

indicate specific locations. The Chicago shows examplified the latter type of design. Since the three plays were originally planned for a rotating schedule (which did not take place), the basic set was the same for all three: a two foot high platform running across the stage fourteen feet behind the curtain line, with semi-circular steps in front of it. For *Othello,* the basic design motif consisted of four columns upstage on the platform. The City of Cyprus was shown on a drop behind the platform and the columns. With the addition of a table and chairs in front of a curtain covering the permanent platform, the scene shifted to the council chambers. Othello's garden was created with a drop of four cypress trees covering the four columns and two shrubs.[13]

A similar concept was applied to *Hamlet,* where tapestries framed the palace rooms, either in front of the permanent set or including it. The castle battlements were a high platform behind the lower, full stage platform, and the graveyard was played before a translucent drop. *As You Like It* utilized the same set painted in shades of green, with a drop and cut-out trees.[14]

Other Federal Theatre Shakespeare productions generally used a single set throughout. A Boston production of *Macbeth* in 1939, for example, used a large, rocky platform with battlements on top, an archway beneath, and a staircase stage left. Scenes were played on different parts of the stage. *The Merry Wives of Windsor* in Los Angeles, 1939 was played before a cartooned street drop, with props and furniture carried on for each scene.

The FTP 1936 New York *Macbeth*. A soldier. Courtesy the Billy Rose Theatre Collection, the New York Public Library at Lincoln Center, the Astor, Lenox and Tilden Foundations.

San Francisco's *The Taming of the Shrew*, 1936, based its design on Shakespeare's own theatre. The actors performed before a facade with a balcony above, and a curtained off playing area below, which looked very similar to John Crawford Adams' reconstruction of the Globe.

Federal Theatre directors adapted Shakespeare's scripts for their contemporary audiences. With black *Macbeths*, a Fascist *Julius Caesar*, and major cutting and rearrangement of the scripts in most of the productions, the Federal Theatre did not adhere to historical accuracy nor tradition. The primary concern of the directors and actors was to make the plays appeal to their audience. A New Orleans newspaper headline of August 4, 1936 read, "Romeo's Juliet Finds Her Nurse Was A Mammy." The article lays out the specifics of the production:

> *A modernized New Orleans version of the play* Romeo and Juliet *with a negro mammy . . . filling the part of the old nurse, death of the lovers in a tomb in Old St. Louis cemetery and their first meeting at a carnival ball — this is an adaptation . . . for the Federal Theatre's next play. "The iron grill balconies of the French Quarter will lend themselves beautifully to the balcony scene," [the adaptor] said with enthusiasm.*[15]

New York City's Negro *Macbeth* was a truly startling production. On March 14, 1936, New York audiences found the Scottish tragedy set in a tropical spot resembling Haiti. Orson Welles, the director, and John Houseman, the producer, felt that "the witch element of the play [fell] beautifully into the supernatural atmosphere of Haitian voodooism."[16] The story of Macbeth's rise and fall, they felt, reflected the revolutionary times of Henri Christophe, the "Negro King of Haiti."

In adapting the script for his black performers, Welles emphasized the supernatural elements of the play. He used a troupe of African drummers in the witch scenes, and changed the Scottish witches into voodoo witch doctors. He took a number of the witches' lines and pulled them together in the character of Hecate, the leader of the witches, who commanded with a ten foot long bullwhip.[17]

Most of the action took place in the courtyard of Macbeth's castle. Other scenes, like the witches scenes and the scene with Macduff, were played before drops in front of the castle. Nat Karson, who designed both the scenery and costumes, dressed the soldiers in exaggerated nineteenth century military uniforms, complete with foot-long epaulets. One reviewer noted that "the gentle Bard of Avon is bedecked with voodoo dances, tom-toms, savage noises, strange writhings and as fine a set of fancy dress ball uniforms as ever dazzles an audience in the theatre."[18] For Burns Mantle the production was not authentic Shakespeare, yet he wrote, "it was weirdly fascinating in color and action. It whipped up considerable excitement in jungle scenes peopled by a whole stageful of witches and a chorus of voodoo assistants."[19]

This staging was one of the most popular and best known of the Federal Theatre's productions. Critics praised its originality and audiences, both black

The FTP 1937 Los Angeles *Macbeth*. A costume sketch for Lady Macbeth. Courtesy the Library of Congress Federal Theatre Project Collection, at George Mason University Libraries, Fairfax, Virginia.

and white, flocked to Harlem during its four month run in New York. The production toured the country for another two and a half months.

In July 1937, the Los Angeles Project, influenced by the popularity of the New York production, did their own black version of *Macbeth*, set in Africa. The producers were promised a copy of the Welles adaptation, but when it failed to arrive by the beginning of rehearsals, they prepared their own version. (Only after it was finished did the Welles script arrive.)[20]

As in the Welles production, the role of the supernatural was increased and Hecate, the witch lord, plays a major role in the action. The Los Angeles producers retained this from the Welles version. It was theatrically effective and they were paying royalties on Welles' adaptation.

This *Macbeth* established a savage jungle mood through its sets, costumes and lighting. Abyssinia and Madagascar were used as the basis for the designs. The main set was the palace courtyard: an open area surrounded ominously by walls and towers. A scrim and flat pieces of African design on bamboo posts covering the palace were used for the jungle, Duncan's encampment, and the sea coast.[21]

The African motif was carried out in the costumes as well. The costumes were simple, but used ornate headdresses, and ornaments made of feathers, beads, tubing and carved wooden animal teeth. The costume report gave this description:

> *The costumes were inspired by those of Madagascar, the Congo regions and Abbysinia. The materials used were muslins, percales, desert cloth and linine, never velvets or silk.*
>
> *The applied design suggested tapacloth and in all cases was executed with bold strokes. Stripes were wide and contrasting in color. . . . Where the costumes were kept simple — attention was centered on the headdresses and ornaments. Carved wooden teeth of animals were plentifully used as were feathers, copper, brass and silver wire, flat metal and rows of cloth tubing sewn together to simulate massive bracelets and collars of metal.*[22]

The melodrama, as well as the supernatural elements and the exotic locations, was emphasized. According to one critic, audiences could see "the familiar classic, set in the African jungles, chilling one's blood with savage rhythms, pistol shots, and sibilant tom-toms." He felt that the poetry took second place to the spectacle, and found the mood of the play to be "fear and impending doom; and to this end, the screaming voices, the clutching apparitions, the shadowy scenery contribute forcefully."[23] Another review noted that the "Speeches are intensified in mood by music or with shouts and cries from the wings. At all times the stage is an intensely animated picture. Writhing bodies, clutching hands and swift movement of groups from one side to another play an important part in heightening the melodramatic effect."[24]

The critical response was generally good. The cast was often praised for their acting and criticized for their diction. However, some reviewers did

The FTP 1937 Los Angeles *Macbeth*. Jess Lee Brooks as Macbeth and Mae Turner as Lady Macbeth. Courtesy the Library of Congress Federal Theatre Project Collection, at George Mason University Libraries, Fairfax, Virginia.

not like the adaptation. The *Los Angeles Evening News* felt it was "ridiculous to hear savages addressing each other by such fine Scots names as Banquo, Macbeth, Duncan and MacDuff [sic]."[25] A critic for the *Los Angeles Evening Herald and Express* wrote:

> *Considered as an African version of Shakespeare, Federal Theatre's production of* Macbeth *. . . may be called a magnificent failure. . . . it had been given the most spectacular staging lately seen in any Federal show, if not in any productions outside of the movies. . . . Such things and the bald outline of the action may suffice for some, but not for me, who sees no excuse for this gory melodrama unless for the part Shakespeare put into it. Far better present a theme and story native to the background of the African people than this hybrid version of an Anglo-Saxon show.*[26]

One of the most interesting productions of a Shakespeare play by the Federal Theatre was the Delaware *Julius Caesar*. The play was presented in modern dress, with Caesar and his followers costumed in Fascist black shirts. The production opened February 10, 1937, almost a year before the premiere of the Mercury Theatre's own modern dress version of *Julius Caesar*.

The production was given a great deal of publicity in the community. Both the costuming and the staging were considered very novel. According to the Wilmington *Journal Every Evening*,

> *Never before, so far as can be determined, has Shakespeare's* Julius Caesar *been given a modern dress production. True to the traditions of the Elizabethan stage, the audience and players will be drawn more closely together by having much of the action off the stage and in the aisles.*[27]

Robert Schnitzer, director of the Delaware Federal Theatre, wrote that the production had two main purposes: "By its parallel to current events to show that human nature remains basically the same, regardless of time; and to prove that Shakespeare is still 'good theatre,' even without fancy dress costumes."[28]

Schnitzer used several devices to bring the audience closer to the action. Actors delivered the speeches to the crowd directly at the audience. Processions passed among the spectators, and some actors were seated in the aisle. During the famous oration scene, Antony occupied the stage alone, with Caesar's body in a bronze casket. The crowd mingled with the audience and Antony lit a cigarette for emphasis after his funeral oration.[29]

The novel aspect of this production was the modern dress, or more specifically, the parallel it drew between the historical dictator and the current Italian leader, Mussolini. El Thompson, playing Caesar, even resembled Mussolini. Pictures of Thompson in costume were run in the papers with headlines such as "No, Not Il Duce."[30] The designer described the modern dress costumes:

The FTP 1937 Los Angeles *Macbeth*. Hecate and witches. Courtesy the Library of Congress Federal Theatre Project Collection, at George Mason University Libraries, Fairfax, Virginia.

> *The citizens wear street dress, of course. The soothsayer may be a woman dressed as a gypsy fortune teller. Caesar wears blackshirt, breeches, boots, Sam Brown belt and is surrounded by the same. The conspirators wear blackshirt at first, but after the assassination they change to khaki military unifroms to distinguish the faction of democracy from Marc Antony and Octavius who remain in blackshirt.*[31]

The theatre in which the play was produced had a very small stage area and therefore the set was quite economical. The first act used a center upstage arch and side arches on each side, with colored backings behind the center arch to change the locale. The second act set used only the side arches with an outdoor drop and wooden wings. Drapes were used as tents.[32] Because of the small stage area, the processions and crowd scenes were done in the auditorium. Minor characters were cut and a number of short scenes were omitted.[33]

The production was very successful, with reviews praising the acting and directing. One critic even apologized in his review for his earlier derision of the modern dress concept. Remembering the production years later,

The FTP 1937 Los Angeles *Macbeth*. Jess Lee Brooks as Macbeth and the three witches. Courtesy the Library of Congress Federal Theatre Project Collection, at George Mason University Libraries, Fairfax, Virginia.

The FTP 1937 Los Angeles *Macbeth*. Palace set rendering by designer Frederick Stover. Courtesy the Library of Congress Federal Theatre Project Collection, at George Mason University Libraries, Fairfax, Virginia.

Schnitzer, the director, wrote that the cast did "a splendid job."[34]

The play influenced even those who did not see it. The Rev. J. Francis Tucker of St. Anthony's Roman Catholic Church, in a letter to the editor of *The Morning Star*, took exception to the comparison of the tyrant Caesar with Mussolini, who in the Reverend's opinion had done great things for Italy. He refused an invitation to see the show. Naturally the publicity increased attendance.[35]

The production gained attention throughout the entire Federal Theatre Project and a modern dress *Julius Caesar* was scheduled for the classical unit in New York City for the next season. In June 1937, the directors of that unit, John Houseman and Orson Welles, however, left the Project in a dispute over *The Cradle Will Rock*. *Cradle* became the premiere presentation of their Mercury Theatre, which for its first season produced several shows originally slated for the Federal Theatre, including Welles' famous modern dress *Julius Caesar*.[36]

Another production which reflected the political climate was the Roslyn, Long Island, *Coriolanus*. A program note called it "Shakespeare's 'timely' play," and also mentioned "its possible application to current events and world characters."[37] This show exemplified many of the characteristics of

The FTP 1937 Delaware *Julius Caesar*. Act I. "Hail Caesar!" Scenery and costume designs by Ben Edwards. Courtesy the Library of Congress Federal Theatre Project Collection, at George Mason University Libraries, Fairfax, Virginia.

the Federal Theatre's approach to Shakespeare in scenery, staging and concept.

The production was not modernized, like the Delaware *Julius Caesar*. Instead, Charles Hopkins, the director, tried to give the play what the production notes call a universal quality, from no specific time period.[38] The setting, designed by Ben Edwards, was a modern unit set with steps leading from the center aisle on through to the back of the stage. Pylons served as wings of a sort and gray curtains between them were used to change the locale.[39]

Although the costuming, also designed by Ben Edwards, strove for a universal effect, the *New York Post* noted "a compromise between the Elizabethan and the Roman style." Both the costumes and the scenery, however, were praised in many reviews. The *Northport Observer* critic said, "[Ben Edwards'] costumes are a glory of color and effectiveness while the stage setting is at once imaginative, modernistic and lovely to the eye."[40]

This production was also staged to involve the audience. According to reviews, Hopkins had "Spear carrying soldiers with trumpeters and kettle drummers parade up and down both center aisles . . . and actors harangue the orchestra patrons as if they were a mob on the stage. . . . "[41]

The play was first presented in Long Island in October 1937 and received enthusiastic critical notices.[42] A full house cheered the opening night perfor-

The FTP 1937 Delaware *Julius Caesar*. El Thompson as Caesar and Lucille Anderson as Calpurnia. Courtesy the Library of Congress Federal Theatre Project Collection, at George Mason University Libraries, Fairfax, Virginia.

mance and gave the players ten curtain calls. In February 1938, the play was brought to New York City with three other Roslyn productions for a New York State festival. Running at the time in New York was the Mercury Theatre modern dress *Julius Caesar*. As the *World Telegram* put it, "these persistent revivals are making out the Bard as quite a political commentator these days." Comparisons were inevitable. Burns Mantle found "*Coriolanus* the better Shakespeare, but the *Julius Caesar*, the more exciting production."[43] The final sentences of this review give adequate appraisal of the work of this company and the Federal Theatre in general:

> *I think the people should be proud of their theatre as it is represented in this revival, particularly in the work of the actors. Here, in this Roslyn repertory built up by the New York State Unit, we have a return to much that was best in the old stock company era.*

One of the most successful productions of Shakespeare by the Federal Theatre was *The Merchant of Venice* presented in Los Angeles in 1937. Robert Henderson, the director, approached the play as a "comedy of carnival time."[44] He wanted to present "the glitter of Venice in all its glory," and included an "orchestra, an elaborate musical score and carnival dances from the commedia dell'arte."[45]

Henderson emphasized the Portia-Bassanio love story, with Shylock as a melodramatic background. He took what he considered a novel approach to Shylock. The moneylender was played as an exaggerated villain, dressed in red hair and wig (which, according to the producers was the practice in Shakespeare's time), and presented as a man of about forty-five, a vigorous man, not an ancient fool.[46] According to the Los Angeles *Illustrated Reflector* the show was considered innovative for its time:

> *For the first time in the history of the American theatre a Negro actor has been selected to play the important role of the Prince of Morocco in Shakespeare's immortal* The Merchant of Venice.[47]

Jess Lee Brooks who had played Macbeth in Los Angeles portrayed the Moroccan Prince. The cast also boasted Gareth Hughes as Shylock and Estelle Winwood, making a guest appearance with the project, as Portia. At the time, Miss Winwood was a popular stage and screen actress. She was also a good friend of Henderson's. Hughes had acted in films since 1919, and performed onstage in both England and the United States.[48]

According to the designer, "The settings were created to enhance the luxury and gaiety of the play; like an Italian Court play, great color was brought into the costumes. Throughout there was an atmosphere of beauty and color." The basic color scheme was a dark gold bronze which shaded into brown, with red, brown, blue and olive green as accents. The production utilized one basic set that was altered for changing scenes. Different panels were used in the backdrop for different scenes, and the street scenes were played before drops.[49] Henderson departed from one almost univer-

The FTP 1937 Los Angeles *The Merchant of Venice*. Estelle Winwood as Portia and Bassanio. Courtesy the Library of Congress Federal Theatre Project Collection, at George Mason University Libraries, Fairfax, Virginia.

sal Federal Theatre practice: he left most of Shakespeare's text intact.[50]

The production was an unqualified success. The critics were very generous in their praise. It was considered the best production of the Los Angeles Federal Theatre, and Jess Lee Brooks, Gareth Hughes and Estelle Winwood were all singled out for special praise.[51] The director's notes mentioned another tribute he received: "Max Reinhardt said it was the finest performance and production of the play he had seen in thirty years."[52]

Public performances were not the only productions of Shakespeare's plays by the Federal Theatre. Realizing that its commitment to building audiences began with young people, the Federal Theatre produced many shows for children and teen-agers. Among these were several of Shakespeare's plays.

In the spring of 1936, a production of *Twelfth Night* toured the schools, churches and communities in and around Boston. In Los Angeles in 1938, Gareth Hughes arranged a program of scenes including the queen's closet scene from *Hamlet*, the trial scene from *The Merchant of Venice*, and scenes from *Richard II*.[53] In Detroit, the Detroit Federal Theatre presented *The Merry Wives of Windsor* primarily for schools with twenty-nine performances and 13,231 paid admissions.[54] In the spring of 1938, the New York City unit produced a shortened version of *Coriolanus*, which was taken to interested schools. The production, which ran only fifty minutes and used a very simple set, played to large audiences. The favorable response warranted the formation of the Classical Program for High Schools. *Macbeth* was the first play of the 1938-1939 season (and the only Shakespeare play of the four presented). The Classical Program played to 68,175 people in eighty-four performances. A second season was being readied when the Federal Theatre Project was shut down on June 30, 1939.[55]

For Hallie Flanagan, the Federal Theatre Project's purpose did not end with relief. It only began there. It went far beyond it in an attempt to create contemporary regional theatres. The Shakespeare productions were not only part of a large scale program that brought work to approximately ten thousand people, but also part of one of the most exciting theatrical ventures of the century. The Shakespeare productions of the Federal Theatre Project illustrate a unique approach to Shakespearean interpretation in script adaptations, production designs and concepts, and casting. They reflect the artistic and political climate of an important era in American theatre history.

## NOTES

[1]Hallie Flanagan, *Arena* (New York: Duell, Sloan and Pearce, 1940), p. 188. Also see Tony Buttitta and Barry Witham, *Uncle Sam Presents: A Memoir of the Federal Theatre, 1935-1939* (Philadelphia: Univ. of Pennsylvania Press, 1982), and John O'Connor and Lorraine Brown, eds., *Free, Adult, Uncensored: The Living History of the Federal Theatre Project* (Washington, D.C.: New Republic Books, 1978).

[2]Flanagan, p. 432; and Comprehensive Record of Federal Theatre productions at the Research Center for the Federal Theatre, George Mason University, Fairfax, Virginia.

[3]Production Comments, production bulletin: *Coriolanus*, Roslyn, Long Island, G. M. U.

[4]Director's Report, production bulletin: *The Taming of the Shrew*, San Francisco, G. M. U., and the National Archives.

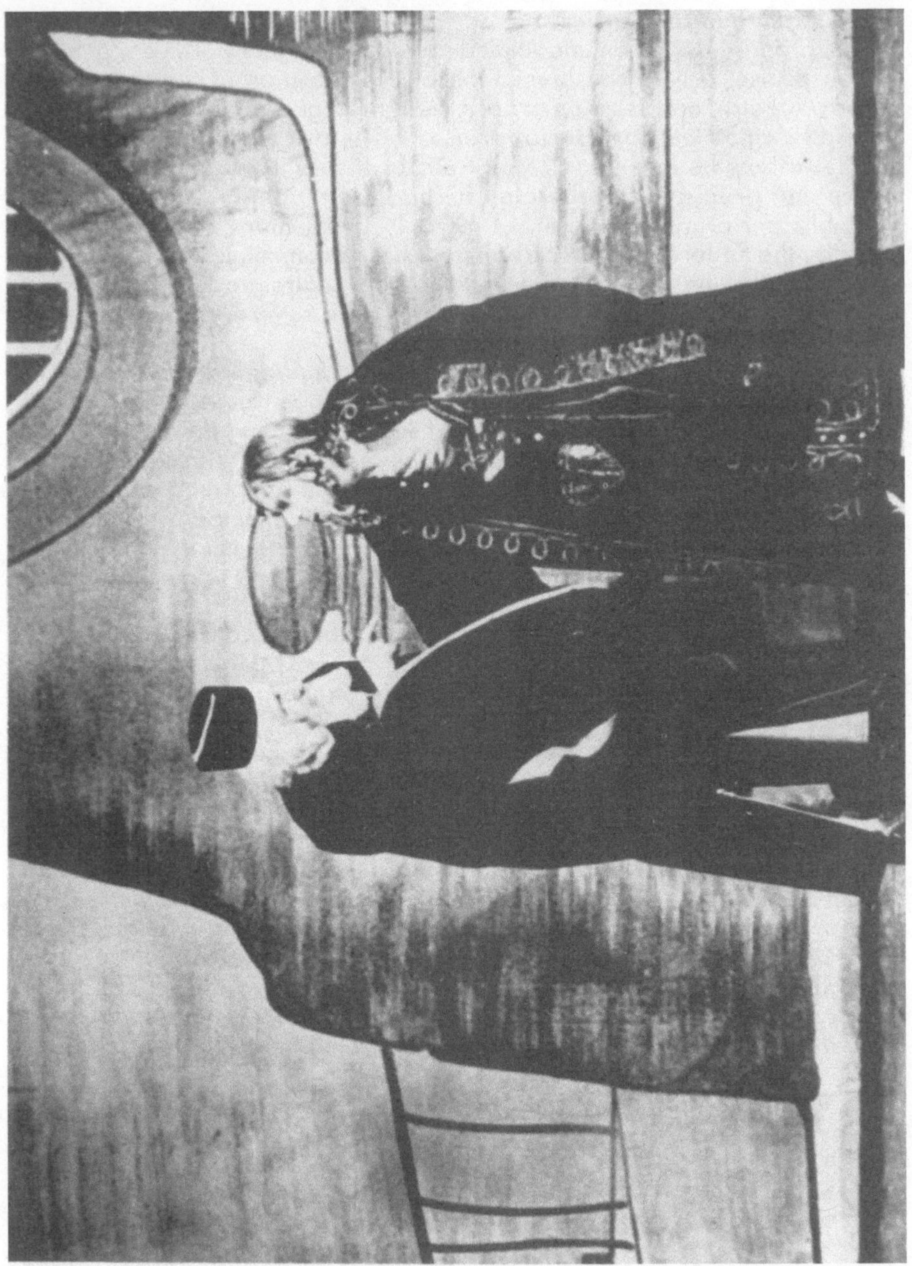

The FTP 1937 Los Angeles *The Merchant of Venice*. Gareth Hughes as Shylock and Tubal. Courtesy the Library of Congress Federal Theatre Project Collection, at George Mason University Libraries, Fairfax, Virginia.

[5]Excerpt from a taped interview of Robert Schnitzer by John O'Connor, November 17, 1975. (This is one in a series of tapes in the Oral History library at the Research Center for the Federal Theatre Project, G. M. U.) Flanagan, p. 258.

[6]Chicago *Daily News*, March 25, 1939, in "Federal Theatre Clippings: Illinois, March-May 1939," N. A.

[7]Chicago *Daily News*, April 20, 1939; and Director's Report, production bulletin: *Shakespeare Repertoire*, Chicago, N. A. and G. M. U.

[8]Chicago *Daily News*, April 20, 1939.

[9]Chicago *Daily News*, and *Chicago American*, April 12, 1939.

[10]Chicago *Daily Times*, May 4, 1939.

[11]Chicago *Daily News*, June 8, 1939; and Chicago *Daily Tribune*, June 9, 1939.

[12]Flanagan, p. 321.

[13]Designer's Report: *Shakespeare Repertoire*.

[14]Designer's Report: *Shakespeare Repertoire*.

[15]New Orleans *States*, August 4, 1936, in "Federal Theatre Clippings: Iowa, Louisiana, Maine, 1936-1937," N. A.

[16]*New York Times*, April 5, 1936, in "Federal Theatre Press Clippings: New York City, January-April 1936," N. A.

[17]John Houseman, *Run Through* (New York: Simon and Schuster, 1972), p. 190.

[18]Unidentified clipping by William F. McDermott, March 14, 1936, in "Federal Theatre Clippings: New York City, January-April 1936."

[19]New York *Daily News*, April 15, 1936.

[20]Director's Report, production bulletin: *Macbeth*, Los Angeles, N. A. and G. M. U.

[21]Director's Report and Technical Report, production bulletin.

[22]Costume Report, production bulletin.

[23]*Script*, July 31, 1937.

[24]Los Angeles *Examiner*, July 15, 1937, in "Federal Theatre Clippings: Southern California, July 1937," N. A.

[25]Los Angeles *Evening News*, July 15, 1937.

[26]Los Angeles *Evening Herald and Express*, July 14, 1937.

[27]Wilmington *Journal Every Evening*, February 4, 1937, in "Federal Theatre Clippings: Delaware, Georgia, 1936-1937," N. A.

[28]General Note, production bulletin: *Julius Caesar*, Delaware, G. M. U.

[29]Directing Notes, production bulletin; and Wilmington *Journal Every Evening*, February 11, 1937.

[30]Wilmington *Journal Every Evening*, February 4, 1937.

[31]Costume Notes, production bulletin.

[32]Technical Report, production bulletin.

[33]Cutting and Arrangement, and Directing Notes, production bulletin.

[34]Wilmington *Journal Every Evening*, February 11, 1937; and Robert C. Schnitzer, personal letter to Stephen M. Vallillo, June 2, 1977.

[35]Flanagan, p. 259, and Delaware clippings of February 14, 1937 and following.

[36]Jane DeHart Matthews, *The Federal Theatre 1935-1939* (Princeton: Princeton University Press, 1967), p. 165. See also *Run Through* which tells a great deal about not only the choice of the play for the Mercury season but also the split with the Project and the production itself.

[37]Program, production bulletin: *Coriolanus*, Roslyn, Long Island.

[38]Production Comment, production bulletin.

[39]New York *Sun*, February 2, 1938, in "New York 1936, Roslyn Theatre of the Four Seasons, Press Clippings, Book Three," filed under the category of National Service Bureau Technical Department — Blueprints, Designs and Photographs, N.A.

[40]New York *Post*, February 3, 1938, New York *World Telegram*, February 2, 1938, and Northport *Observer*, October 15, 1937.

[41]*Brooklyn Eagle*, February 2, 1938 and New York Home News, February 3, 1938, in "Federal Theatre Clippings: New York City, February 1-15, 1938," N. A.

[42]Northport *Observer*, October 15, 1937.

[43]New York *World Telegram*, February 2, 1938, and New York *Daily News*, February 3, 1938.

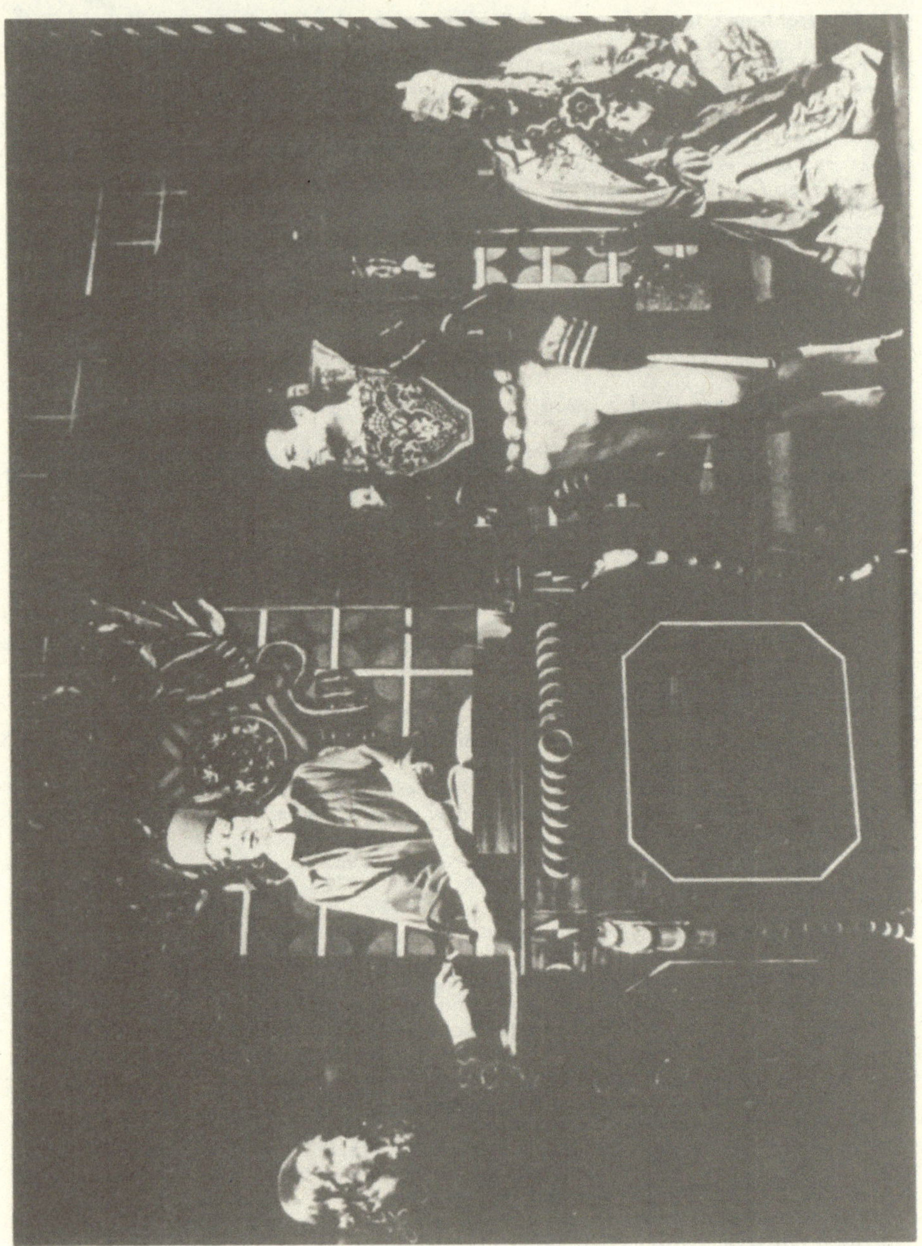

The FTP 1937 Los Angeles *The Merchant of Venice*. Gareth Hughes as Shylock, Estelle Winwood as Portia, Antonio, and the Duke of Venice. Courtesy the Library of Congress Federal Theatre Project Collection, at George Mason University Libraries, Fairfax, Virginia.

[44]Director's Report, production bulletin: *The Merchant of Venice*, Los Angeles, N. A. and G. M. U.

[45]Los Angeles *Press*, March 22, 1937, in "Federal Theatre Clippings: Southern California, March 1937," N. A.

[46]Director's Report, production bulletin.

[47]Los Angeles *Illustrated Reflector*, March 17, 1937.

[48]Los Angeles *Press*, February 10, 1936, in "Federal Theatre Clippings: Southern California, January, February, March 1936," N. A.

[49]Director's Report and Technical Report, production bulletin.

[50]Director's Report, production bulletin.

[51]Los Angeles *Examiner*, March 26, 1937, and Los Angeles *Evening News*, March 26, 1937.

[52]Director's Report, production bulletin.

[53]Letter from C. W. Sandifur, November 21, 1938, in file "Letters of Commendation," Federal Theatre Project Testimonial Letters, Box 109; and Los Angeles *Daily News*, May 6, 1938, in "Federal Theatre Clippings: Southern California, May 1938," N. A.

[54]Stage Manager's Report, production bulletin: *The Merry Wives of Windsor*, Detroit, G. M. U.

[55]"An Analysis of the Classical Program," and "The Classical Program for High Schools," leaflets in the file "Classical Program — High Schools," New York City (National Office) Correspondence File, Box 2, N. A.

Miss Louisa Missouri as Alice Darvil in *Ernest Maltravers*. From Odell, *Annals. . .*, IV, opp. 224.

# Theatre and Narrative Fiction in the Work of the Nineteenth-Century American Playwright Louisa Medina

ROSEMARIE K. BANK

Rarely does research uncover an historical figure both significant and unknown. There are scattered references to Louisa Medina in one or two biographies of actors or of the novelists whose works she adapted, and in the theatrical histories of Ireland, Brown, and Odell. The largest amount of information about her, however, has remained locked for over a hundred and fifty years in the periodicals and dailies that published New York theatrical information. Today, we will exhume the historical record insofar as it pertains to Louisa Medina's dramatizations of novels, and ask the following questions: what were Medina's playwriting techniques, why did her plays persist where other adaptations from the same sources disappeared, and what is the importance of her work to American theatrical history?

According to an interview she gave during her lifetime, Louisa Medina was born about 1813 in Europe. Her father was a Spanish businessman who went bankrupt, leaving his daughter with sufficient relatives and/or money to acquire an education, including the dead languages, logic, and algebra. She claimed a successful contribution to a London annual at the age of twelve, and reported spending her years from 14 to 17 traveling and studying in Ireland, France, and Spain. In 1831 or 1833, she first came to America, worked in New York as a teacher of French and Spanish, and began to contribute poems and stories to journals and plays to the theatre.[1] Medina is credited with the authorship of 34 plays between 1833 and 1838, of which 11 can be documented from the historical record.[2] The rest of the works, which have not yet been and perhaps cannot be substantiated, could include translations from novels or even plays which did not appear under Medina's name, such as the adaptation of Scribe's *The Jewess* (March 7, 1836) with which Ireland credits her.[3] None of her obituary notices state her age, but if the information she gave during her lifetime is true, Louisa Medina was 25 when she died of apoplexy in New York on November 12, 1838.

Louisa Medina's plays are all associated with Thomas S. Hamblin, a successful English actor and manager of the Bowery Theatre from 1830. His private life and personality made enemies within the partisan press of the day, and these Medina, whom Hamblin perhaps married in 1837, inherited.[4] In addition, some journals damned anything populist, others anything melodramatic, while other journals simply ran columns of theatrical gossip

Rosemarie K. Bank's articles on American Theatre have appeared in *Theatre Journal, Theatre Survey, Theatre Studies,* and *Theatre History Studies,* etc.

untempered by any attempt at truth or impartiality. Ireland, Odell, and to a lesser extent Brown, have drunk perforce from the records of that time and thus imbibed distortion with fact. The waters can be clarified only by immersing one's self in the record long enough to discover which way the critical tides were running.[5]

Though only three of her known plays appear to have survived, all published years after her death, Louisa Medina is credited with writing and adapting more plays for the American theatre than any other women writer of her time.[6] Lester Wallack said that Medina "was one of the most brilliant women I ever met. She was very plain, but a wonderfully bright woman, charming in every way."[7] Playwriting was Medina's only professional tie to the theatre, and her documented plays consist solely of dramatizations of novels, a goodly part of the early nineteenth-century American repertory.

Louisa Medina's playwriting techniques varied somewhat from work to work, but consisted in "seizing the most prominent points of a story and putting them into a dramatic shape, and while she rarely mutilated the original plot, [she] contrived to throw a deeper interest and effect over the whole."[8] Medina's dramatization of Thomas Fay's *Norman Leslie* in 1836 was praised "for more than mere adaptation. In several instances she has ingeniously contrived to strengthen the original plot, and the effective and declamatory dialogues are creditable to her powers of original composition."[9] An article in 1837 observed that

> *remembering as we do how poorly any of Sir Walter Scott's ecquisite [sic] novels have ever been pourtrayed [sic] upon the stage, we ascribe the success of Miss Medina's plays wholly to the liberties she takes with the authors. A quick knowledge of stage effect shows her at once that which would fail of presenting in one picture to an audience what long pages of elaborate description represents to the reader, and also teaches her that those fine shades of character which interest most in the closet, will fail of striking on the stage.*[10]

Shortly after the opening of *Ernest Maltravers* in 1838, the *Mirror* observed that Medina's

> *power of composition is said to be astonishingly rapid. She is partial to startling and terrible catastrophes. Her knowledge of stage effect is very great, and there is an impassioned ardor in her poetry, which enhances the thrilling interest of her pieces. It has been objected to them that their story departs from that of the novels on which some of them are based; and this objection, as we think, redounds to her praise, for it is an evidence of the fertility of her invention — which is one of the highest attributes of true genius.*[11]

The closest thing to a negative review of her work is the somewhat vague observation in *The Spirit of the Times* that "Bowery audiences have enjoyed [an especial treat] during the week — the non-performance of *Rienzi, Nor-*

*man Leslie,* and other gags, a treat only appreciated by sensible people who have seen those fanfaranades of dramatic flummery."[12]

A comparison of Medina's *Last Days of Pompeii, Nick of the Woods,* and *Ernest Maltravers* to their novel sources by Edward Bulwer-Lytton and Robert Montgomery Bird demonstrates without much difficulty that her plays are indeed more interesting, stronger in plot line and dialogue, and more thrilling than their novels. The plays are entirely stageworthy and if they descend to dramatic flummery, it is where the playwright has too assiduously followed the content or style of the novelists. The chief villain of all three novels is superfluous verbiage and a narrative broken by repeated intrusions of the author's persona.[13] In their subjects, *The Last Days of Pompeii, Nick of the Woods,* and *Ernest Maltravers* represent the three types Medina dramatized: the historical subject (*Pompeii, O'Neill, Rienzi, Lafitte*), the American frontier subject (*Wacousta, Kairrissah, Nick*), and the contemporary romance/adventure subject (*Norman Leslie, Maltravers, Statue Fiend, The Collegians*).

Bulwer-Lytton's *Last Days of Pompeii* grew out of an on-site visit and is heavily indebted to the archeological scholarship of its day. The narrative rockets back and forth between the story of Glaucus and Ione beset by the machinations of the evil Arbaces, and the buildings, customs, artifacts, bodies, etc., uncovered at Pompeii, or the author's view of modern Italy. It is the novelist's purpose to portray the "heated and feverish civilization" of a Pompeii given wholly to pleasure,[14] for the novel exists to illustrate Pompeii, not the other way round. Medina's three-act play concentrates solely on the story of Glaucus and Ione, which with its baths, feasts, games, erotic religious ceremonies, boat trips, mysterious witches, and gladiatorial games, not to omit the earthquake itself, provided ample opportunity for the spectacle the Bowery did so well. Moreover, the story is full of the betrayals, jealousies, misunderstandings, dangers, and would-be seductions beloved by melodramatists.[15] The play's pseudo-Shakespearian dialogue is in places a direct transfer of lines in the novel, but primarily simply a copy of its style, for we must bear in mind that the "peculiar language" of melodrama is peculiar only to our ears, and in its day was simply "literary language."[16]

Bird's *Nick of the Woods, or the Jibbenainosay* features "characters in some instances . . . built on actual people"[17] Bird observed on a western trip, with the rest of the novel drawn from tales about frontier life. Virulently anti-Indian,[18] the bulk of the novel concerns Kentucky and its people in 1782, into which has been woven the story of Roland and his cousin Edith Forrester. The novel gives us a double villain — a deceased uncle who disliked Roland and Edith and his evil agent Braxley who gets them disinherited. The hero of the piece is not Roland, a hopeless woodsman, but a forest-savy Quaker, Nathan, who is in truth the dread Indian killer, the Jibbenainosay. To him is added Roaring Ralph Stackpole, a horse thief who provides endless examples of frontier brag speech, very much in vogue in the 1830's,[19] a militia officer to exemplify frontier kindness and gaucherie, Wenonga the fiendish Indian chief and Nathan's nemesis, and Tellie Doe, the gentle daughter of a renegade white man. Medina's three-act play keeps all these

Thomas S. Hamblin in the role of Arbaces in *The Last Days of Pompeii*. From Odell, *Annals*. . . , IV, opp. 38.

characters, muting the evil uncle to a shadow and unfortunately cutting Peter, Nathan's trick dog.

Bird's novel is far less eventful than *The Last Days of Pompeii* and Medina's work consisted of tightening the central plot around the disputed legacy. In the novel, the dead uncle had an illegitimate daughter in whose name Braxley claims the Virginia estate, implying Tellie Doe is the girl. This is reversed in the last chapters, where the daughter is revealed to have died in infancy. In the play, Tellie Doe, not Edith, is the star part, a brave forest maiden who knocks the villain down and tries to save the feckless Roland and Edith from Braxley, the rampaging Indians, and their own stupidity. In the play, Tellie really is the uncle's daughter, born of a secret marriage, but Medina kills her off at the end of the play while defending Roland, whom she secretly loves, thereby clearing the way for Roland and Edith to return to an undisputed inheritance in Virginia.[20] Similarly, in the nove. the Jibbenainosay moves on to other frontiers, while in the play, his revenge complete, he dies. Simplifying the legacy question leaves Medina ample room for raging cataracts, canoes of fire precipitated over waterfalls, daring rescues from bridges dangling over rocky passes, plus songs, scenes at the Indian camp, and the rest of the beloved paraphernalia of the frontier novel and play.

Bulwer-Lytton's novel *Ernest Maltravers* was created to present the author's philosophical views, as he confessed in the 1851 preface to *Alice*, the novel's sequel:

> *The more ingenious and attentive will perhaps perceive that under the outward story, which knits together the destinies of Alice and Maltravers, there is an interior philosophical design. . . . Thus regarded, Ernest Maltravers will appear to the reader as the type of Genius, or Intellectual Ambition, which, at the onset of its career, devots itself with extravagance and often erring passion to Nature alone (typified by Alice) . . . . Completing, however, his mental education in the actual world, . . . [Genius] reunites itself to the Nature from which life and art had for a while distracted it; but to Nature in a higher and more spiritual form than that under which youth beholds it.*[21]

"The outward story" brings together teenaged Ernest Maltravers and Alice Darvil, he son of a nobleman, she daughter of a robber from whose clutches she saves Ernest. Maltravers, under a false name, educates and shelters Alice and they become lovers. While he's away, Alice is kidnapped by and escapes from her father, has Ernest's baby, and subsequently finds a benefactress who sets her up as a music teacher. Maltravers, unable to trace Alice, takes refuge in travel, discourse, writing literature, and politics. The evil father, Darvil, is killed by the police and Alice marries, in name only, after overhearing Ernest in a compromising conversation. Despite mutual friends and several near misses, Ernest and Alice never meet again in the novel, she occupying the next dozen years with domestic pursuits, and he with a tragic infatuation, Parliament, philosophy, and travel. The resolution of their story may be found in Bulwer-Lytton's *Alice,* a sequel not published until years after Medina's death.

Despite the novel's popularity, the prospect of an illicit love affair, pages of philosophy, and a story left hanging may have daunted other dramatizers.[22] Medina retained the central characters and the opening scene where Alice rescues Ernest from her father, but little else. In the play, Ernest and Alice are secretly married, but Ernest, misled by a false friend as to Alice's character, asks her to pretend she's his mistress. This Alice refuses to do,[23] and goes to Maltravers Hall to make herself known, only to interrupt her father, Richard Darvil, in a robbery, in the course of which her father-in-law is killed and Alice told by Darvil she and Ernest are brother and sister.[24] The last of the play's three acts moves from England to Italy's Lake Como, which Bulwer-Lytton described in detail in the novel. Here, replete with lake, singing boaters, and a mountain defile, we find a mad Alice roaming the hills with her bandit father. Ernest appears with friends and all is happily resolved via a letter from Alice's dead mother establishing that Ernest and Alice are first cousins, not brother and sister.

In addition to saving Alice from calumny, Medina rescued a witty and lively female character killed off in the novel, and tried to take the novel's villain from the role of would-be seducer to that of rake reformed. Alice's father, Richard Darvil, the role played by Hamblin and a minor presence in the novel, becomes a central figure in the play and brother to Ernest's father. Given all these changes, the remarks cited earlier to the effect that Medina's play departed significantly from its novel source, appear wholly warranted. One can readily see, moreover, why the "purity" of Medina's writing was noted as a factor in drawing women patrons to the Bowery, but it is less easy, given her choices in dramatizing *Ernest Maltravers,* to see Medina's work as entirely free of "sentimental flim-flam."[25]

Despite their authorship of successful plays, Bulwer-Lytton and Bird declined to dramatize *The Last Days of Pompeii, Nick of the Woods,* or *Ernest Maltravers*. Others were not so hesitant.[26] Of the many versions of *Pompeii* and *Nick,* Medina's was "the abiding adaptation."[27] There do not seem to have been any competing adaptations of *Ernest Maltravers*.[28] No reviews from the 1830's compare Medina's plays unfavorably to rival versions,[29] and the success of her work is well documented. Ireland, Brown, and Odell indicate Medina's longest lived play was *Nick of the Woods,*[30] followed by *Pompeii, Rienzi, Norman Leslie, Ernest Maltravers,* and *Lafitte*. Indeed, after Hamblin's death in 1853, productions of *Pompeii* at the Bowery are recorded as late as 1868, and *Nick* was presented there almost yearly at least to 1882.

Medina's financial arrangements with the Bowery Theatre are not known, but it was the only theatre, barring the 1836-39 fire period, with which she is associated, and Hamblin the only manager of her works. After Medina's death, her most popular plays were revived every year; indeed two, *The Statue Fiend* and *The Collegians,* were first presented posthumously. After Hamblin's death, the Bowery's leading actor and sometime manager Edward Eddy continued to do Medina's plays and to perform roles in them on tour until shortly after the Bowery was sold and passed from Hamblin's heirs in 1867.[31] That Hamblin or Eddy would have repeated Medina's dramatizations for twenty to thirty years after her death if they had lost their power to attract is not likely, since Hamblin dropped many plays he owned, in which he had invested heavily, when they failed to draw. Yet Hamblin had a debt to Medina's plays of long standing, for he had struggled his first five years of management (1830-35), incurring many losses, when engagements by Forrest and Celeste, but particularly the spectacles *Pompeii, Norman Leslie,* and *Rienzi,* enabled Hamblin to pay off his debts and invest in the Bowery.[32] He is said to have cleared $40,000 free of all expenses from the 1835-36 season, the season containing Medina's three biggest hits.[33] Indeed, after Medina's death, Hamblin turned time and again to house playwrights, like J. S. Jones, or to independent authors in an attempt to recapture the successful adaptations Medina had brought him, and Hamblin had produced with what even his enemies grant was great expense and care.

Hamblin studied management at the knee of Charles Gilfert, who, as manager of the first Bowery Theatre is said to have invented press agentry.[34] It was a lesson Hamblin learned well. In his very first season (1830-31), he presented dramatizations of novels — *The Wept of Wish-ton-Wish, Paul Clifford, Cagliostro* — but it was not until *Mazeppa* (July 22, 1883) that Hamblin fully mastered the art of publicizing adaptations. The first Medina dramatizations followed hard upon, and the production history of her plays will lead us in turn to another reason for her success. Examining the data Odell has gathered, we learn:

***Wacousta*** *had a week's uninterrupted run and was "a great hit" (III, p. 679)*

***Kairrissah*** *had an uninterrupted run from Sept. 11 to 17, 1834, and "proved popular (IV, p. 27)*

***Pompeii*** *ran 29 performances with only one interruption through March 7, 1835, the longest run in New York theatrical history to that date, and continued intermittently through the season (IV, p. 31)*

***O'Neill*** *played May 11, 13, 14 and ran in a four-play repertory through May 17, 1835 (IV, p. 34)*

***Norman Leslie*** *ran about 25 performances without interruption until Feb. 7, 1836, without fore or afterpieces until the end of the run, and continued intermittently through the season (IV, pp. 77-80)*

***Rienzi*** *ran about 25 performances without interruption through June 20, 1836, and without fore or afterpiece (IV, pp. 82-83)*

***Lafitte*** *had its straight run interrupted by fire on Sept. 21, 1836 (IV, p. 88)*

***Ernest Maltravers*** *had a week's uninterrupted run, and was revived in April and May, 1838 (IV, pp. 224-225)*

***Nick of the Woods*** *had a week's uninterrupted run, then a broken run at "Flynn's Bowery" until Feb. 12, 1838 (IV, p. 237). In its second premiere,* ***Nick*** *was the opening play at Hamblin's new Bowery Theatre in May, 1839, where it had a week's straight run, and then ran intermittently through August (IV, pp. 316-318)*

***Statue Fiend*** *had a week's uninterrupted run (IV, p. 372)*

***The Collegians*** *played once in 1842 and was withdrawn, to be reintroduced July 3, 1843, for a mixed run until the 18th (IV, p. 634)*

Bearing in mind that a week's uninterrupted run in 1833 was very long and a sign of considerable success, note the awesome prospect of a month's uninterrupted run in 1835 and 1836 for three plays, to which *Lafitte* would surely have been added had the theatre not burned. Moreover, *Ernest Maltravers* and *Nick of the Woods*, which premiered at theatres not under Hamblin's control, would in all likelihood have shared the same fate, for as Odell points out, "The Bowery, before any other theatre in New York, started the custom of continuous runs for successful plays."[35] About *The Statue Fiend* and *The Collegians* it is difficult to speak, since Medina's hand in their presented form cannot be discerned with confidence.

Having considered Medina's playwriting techniques and the persistence of her adaptations over those of her rivals, we are drawn to consider what importance her work has to American theatrical history. Odell remarks, as we have seen, that the Bowery Theatre brought the long, uninterrupted run to New York. We have followed that practice as it pertained to Medina's plays and observed that her work was instrumental to the Bowery's success, indeed survival. As a result of the joint contribution of Hamblin and Medina to the long run, an examination of the received wisdom about that practice may be warranted, in that we are used to dating the long run to the 1840's, citing the one hundred performances of *The Drunkard* in 1844, the forty performances of *Monte Cristo* in 1848-49, and similar production data. It appears, however, that the long, continuous run in U.S. theatrical history can be dated with security to the 1830's and the Bowery Theatre, if not to earlier times and places. In the matter of running plays without fore or afterpieces, Hamblin and Medina may also have been unique. Their contributions, in any case, seem to merit that Thomas Hamblin not be buried in Victorian obloquy because he married several times, his audience ate peanuts in the theatre, or because he brashly boosted American plays and performers. Neither should Louisa Medina's personal relationship to Hamblin cause history to forget she was one of the nineteenth century's few successful woman dramatists, a true woman of letters in her own right, whose work provides an important example of the interplay between theatre and narrative fiction in the United States in the early nineteenth century.[36]

Joseph Proctor in *Nick of the Woods*. From Odell, *Annals*. . . , IV, opp. 310. Originally a lithograph published by Currier and Ives.

**TABLE I**

The plays of Louisa Medina which can be documented from the historical record.

| Title | Date | Source |
|---|---|---|
| *Wacousta, or The Curse* | Dec. 30, 1833 | Major John Richardson's novel (1832) |
| *Kairrissah, or The Warrior of Wanachtiki* | Sept. 11, 1834 | source unknown** |
| *Last Days of Pompeii**** | Feb. 9, 1835 | Edw. Bulwer-Lytton's novel (1834) |
| *O'Neill, the Rebel* | May 11, 1835 | source unknown** |
| *Norman Leslie* | Jan. 11, 1836 | Theo. S. Fay's novel (1835) |
| *Rienzi* | May 23, 1836 | Edw. Bulwer-Lytton's novel (1835) |
| *Lafitte, Pirate of the Gulf* | Sept. 19, 1836 | Jos. Holt Ingraham's novel (1836) |
| *Nick of the Woods**** | Feb. 5, 1838* *(the Bowery when managed for its creditors by Thos. Flynn) May 6, 1839 | Robert Montgomery Bird's novel 1837 |
| *Ernest Maltravers**** | March 28, 1838* *(National, when managed by Wallack) | Edw. Bulwer-Lytton's novel (1837) |
| *The Statue Fiend, or The Curse of the Avenger* | May 18, 1840 | source unknown** |
| *The Collegians* | Dec. 26, 1842/ July 3, 1843 | Gerald Griffin's novel (1829) |

All productions were at the Bowery Theatre under Hamblin's management unless otherwise indicated (*).

**Source unknown means unknown to me at this writing.

****The Last Days of Pompeii* was published in New York in 1856 and is #146 of *French's Standard Drama*.
*Nick of the Woods* was published in Boston in the 1850's and is #62 of *Spencer's Boston Theatre*.
*Ernest Maltravers* was published in London in the 1880's and is #379 of *Dick's Standard Plays*.

(These sources are inventoried by Hixon and Hennessee in their *Nineteenth-Century American Drama: A Finding Guide*.)

## NOTES

[1]*The Spirit of the Times,* Oct. 1, 1836, p. 258. The *Mirror* article cited next dates Medina's arrival in the U.S. to 1831. An article in the *Ladies Companion,* April, 1837 (pp. 301-302), reports Medina had a "masculine and metaphysical" education and supports in a general way the details of her life given in the *Spirit* article.

[2]*The New York Mirror,* April 28, 1838, p. 351. Odell's figure of 31 plays (IV, p. 225) seems to be an error in transcription, since his source is the *Mirror,* which states 34. A list of Medina's eleven documented plays follows these notes.

[3]Joseph Ireland, *Records of the New York Stage from 1750 to 1860,* vol. II (rpt. 1866; New York: Benjamin Blom, 1966), p. 156. The *Ladies Companion* (April, 1837) mentions *The Jewess* as drawn by Medina solely from a London playbill. The article also cites adaptations of Shakespeare's *Pericles* and Spring's novel *Giafar al Barmeki, Il Maledetto,* and *Leona of Athens* as works by Medina.

[4]Lester Wallack, *Memories of Fifty Years* (rpt. 1889; New York: Benjamin Blom, 1969), p. 116. Hamblin and his first wife battled in and out of the press for years. Their divorce decree forbade him to remarry until his first wife died (Odell, IV, pp. 36-37), which she did in 1849, after a long liaison/marriage with a young actor, James S. Charles (Ireland, I, p. 462). Hamblin didn't flaunt the decree, but neither did he obey it, calling Naomi Vincent, who died in childbirth July 30, 1835, at the age of 21, his wife (Ireland, II, p. 22), Louisa Medina his wife, and she is so identified in newspapers and legal records in 1838, and, sometime after Medina's death, the popular actress Mrs. Shaw his wife, though she was not so identified publicly, despite three children, until a year after the death of the first Mrs. Hamblin (Odell, V, p. 538). According to Hamblin's will of Nov. 23, 1836 (HTC), Hamblin and Medina had a daughter, named Louisa Medina Hamblin.

[5]Hamblin's personal life (see note 4) causes Odell to impugn or joke about his "wives" and Ireland marries the personal to the artistic, concluding of Hamblin (I, p. 461): "He was content to fill his purse from such sources, rather than attempt to elevate the drama and its auditors by the production of plays of literary merit and elevated sentiment. His company, generally, was so notoriously incompetent in the better class of plays, and his own character in connection with female reputation so unfortunate, that his theatre was, for years in a double sense, known as the Bowery Slaughter-House." T. A. Brown, in his *A History of the New York Stage, 1732-1901,* vol. I (New York: Dodd, Mead, and Co., 1903), p. 129, counters: "I claim for Thomas Hamblin that he did more for the elevation of the drama in this country than any other man of his time."

[6]*The New York Mirror,* Feb. 20, 1836, p. 270. Medina may have written and had professionally produced more plays than any woman in the nineteenth century. One critic considered her success "the triumph of a woman's genius" (*Mirror,* Aug. 20, 1836, p. 63).

[7]Wallack, p. 119. Medina may be unique in not having combined playwriting with acting or management, as other women in the nineteenth-century theatre did.

[8]Ireland, II, p. 89.

[9]*The New York Mirror,* Jan. 23, 1836, p. 238. The *Mirror* also observed (March 5, 1836, p. 287) that dramatization improved a novel's sales.

[10]*The Ladies Companion and Literary Expositor,* April, 1837, p. 30. This source has been referred to earlier and will be hereafter called simply *The Ladies Companion.*

[11]*The New York Mirror,* April 28, 1838, p. 351. The April 14, 1838, *Mirror* said of Medina's version of *Ernest Maltravers* that "little is taken from the book whose name it bears, all the striking incidents and connecting links of the plot being supplied by the dramatist herself" (p. 334). Of her rapidity of composition, the April, 1837, *Ladies Companion* said (p. 301) that Medina frequently began and completed a finished play in a week and that her version of *Pericles,* judged superior by Sheridan Knowles to John Howard Payne's version, took Medina three days. Yet, the article concluded, "The rapidity of her writing nothing injures its harmony," and supported the assertion with a passage of Medina's verse.

[12]*Spirit of the Times,* Sept. 10, 1836, p. 233.

[13]The preference during the period for a detailed verbal picture in novels led easily to excess, the extent of which may be readily ascertained by comparing the novels mentioned here to, say, the novels of Austen or Dickens.

[14]Edward Bulwer-Lytton, *The Complete Works of Edward Bulwer-Lytton*, vol. 4, *The Last Days of Pompeii* (New York: Kelmscott Society Pubs., n.d.), p. 148.

[15]*The Ladies Companion* of May, 1837, p. 51, reports that the original copy of Medina's *Pompeii* was destroyed when the Bowery burned in 1836, and that she reconstructed the play from two parts (acts?) of it she had saved. Presumably, this is the text that has been preserved. See *The Last Days of Pompeii* (N.Y.: French's Standard Drama #146, 1856).

[16]The point is clearly illustrated in this passage from *Nick of the Woods*, which Medina transferred to her play nearly verbatim from Chapter 1 of the novel:

> *Edith:* *Cousin, will you not forward and salute the friends who are waiting to give us welcome?*
>
> *Roland:* *Us? Where shall we look for friends to give us welcome?*
>
> *Edith:* *Here, among the inhabitants of these woods. A kinder or more hospitable people exist not on earth.*
>
> *Roland:* *I know it, Edith; but to see you, the favored offspring of luxury and wealth, thrown thus upon a savage wild, galls my soul. Are these rough people fit companions for the tender Edith Forrester?*
>
> *Edith:* *They are, Roland. Honesty should be the welcome companion of all. Shall we despond because the treachery of a villain induced our uncle to disinherit us, and who has sent us forth to wander as exiles in a strange land? No! . . .*
>
> *Roland:* *If thou art content, dare I complain?*

See Louisa Medina, *Nick of the Woods* (Boston: Spencer's Boston Theatre #62, n.d.), pp. 4-5.

[17]Clement E. Foust, *The Life and Dramatic Works of Robert Montgomery Bird* (New York: Knickerbocker Press, 1919), pp. 96-97.

[18]Bird explains his sentiments and the response to them in the preface to *Nick of the Woods, or the Jibbenainosay* (New York: W. J. Widdleton Pubs., 1868), pp. iii-vii.

[19]This exchange from Act I of Medina's play (pp. 9-10) captures the novel's use of verbal local color:

> *Ralph:* *Who's for a fight? Where's your old coon can claw the bark off a gum tree? Where's your wolf of the rolling prairies? . . . Ain't I the old snag to shake off a saddle — can go down Old Salt on my back and swim up the Ohio! Hurray for a fight!*
>
> *Roland:* *What a strange medley of the bully and the hero is that man!*

[20]Virtue's reward in the play is Roland's apostrophe for Tellie (p. 28), "Noble-hearted girl! O, woman, woman! In the crowded city, or the silent desert, thou art still the same! Faithful in love, fearless in danger, man's first and last, his surest, truest friend."

[21]Edward Bulwer-Lytton, *The Complete Works of Edward Bulwer-Lytton*, vol. 6, *Ernest Maltravers* and *Alice* (New York: Kelmscott Society Pubs., n.d.), preface to *Alice*, p. ii.

[22]See note 28.

[23]Alice says, "Ernest, my life is yours, if you demand it — my honor is my own." See Louisa Medina, *Ernest Maltravers* (London: Dick's Standard Plays #379, n.d.), p. 19.

[24]I've found no proof that Bulwer-Lytton knew Medina's play, yet he, too, has incest as a theme in *Alice*, in the love affair between Ernest and his and Alice's supposed daughter Evelyn. The novelist, having consigned the once unchaste Alice to a happy ending with Ernest rather than to death, says at the last, "It is time that we should do away with the punishment of death for inadequate offenses, even in books" (*Alice*, p. 369).

[25]*The New York Mirror*, Aug. 20, 1836, p. 63.

[26]A version of *Pompeii* by Edward Fitzball first appeared in London in 1834, another by Charlotte Barnes played at Caldwell's in New Orleans in 1835, there is record of a version by a Mr. Raymond (date unknown), a dramatization by John Oxenford in 1872, and another by James Pain in 1889. *Nick of the Woods* was dramatized by G. W. Harby in New Orleans for the tragedian Edmund S. Conner, there was a version by a western author named Morden,

another version in the Chatham repertory and one at the National, April 1, 1839, "written expressly for this theatre" (Brown, I, p. 251), and yet another version by J. T. Haines was published in England. See Curtis Dahl, *Robert Montgomery Bird* (New York: Twayne Pubs., 1963), p. 91. Information from this source has been incorporated with that from Ireland, Brown, and Odell, who are also the sources for the list of *Pompeii* and *Maltravers* adaptations, or lack of them.

[27]George C. D. Odell, *Annals of the New York Stage*, vol. IV (New York: Columbia University Press, 1928), p. 299. All previous and all further references to Odell are to this source.

[28]Neither Ireland, Brown, nor Odell mention other adaptations of *Ernest Maltravers*, nor have I found references to any in studies of Bulwer-Lytton's work. A possible reason was advanced earlier for no dramatizations except Medina's.

[29]None of the texts of rival versions performed in New York in the 1830's has survived, thus we are thrown solely upon the authority of reviews and critical reports of the day.

[30]The extraordinary longevity of *Nick* must in part be credited to Joseph Proctor, who made a life's work of the Jibbenainosay, the role he created in the 1839 Bowery production. Still, the play was revived in 1921, long after Proctor's death. The long survival of *The Last Days of Pompeii* on the stage was surely aided by its moral triumph of Christianity over paganism.

[31]Brown, I, p. 142.

[32]Odell, III, pp. 518-525, and Brown, I, p. 113. Ireland says of *Rienzi* that it surpassed, "if possible, every spectacular display hitherto attempted in New York. It was triumphantly successful" (II, p. 156).

[33]*Ladies Companion*, June, 1837, p. 96.

[34]Brown, I, p. 105.

[35]Odell, III, p. 515.

[36]I here record my gratitude to Reference Librarian Mark Tucker and to Ruth Rothenberg and her Inter-Library Loan staff, whose skill and helpfulness assisted this research immeasurably. My thanks are also expressed to Martha R. Mahard, Asst. Curator of the Harvard Theatre Collection, for her generous description of Hamblin's papers.

Figure 1. Henry Irving as Becket, in Act I, Scene iii. The Hall in Northampton Castle. By Chas. A. Buchel. From Austin Brereton, *Henry Irving* (London, 1905), opp. p. 48.

# C. V. Stanford's Incidental Music to Henry Irving's Production of Tennyson's *Becket*

**KENNETH DELONG and DENIS SALTER**

In 1876 Tennyson's play *Queen Mary* opened at the Lyceum Theatre. The play itself was a failure, but it accomplished one significant thing: it brought together three men who, some seventeen years later, were to collaborate on one of the greatest successes of Victorian theatre — *Becket*. The three men — Tennyson, Henry Irving, and composer Charles Villiers Stanford — were all eminent Victorians, personal friends, and prominent members of their respective professions, but aside from *Queen Mary, Becket* was their only collaboration.

The initial impetus for *Becket* came from Henry Irving, who, after taking control of the Lyceum Theatre in 1878, asked Tennyson for a new play. After considering several historical subjects, Tennyson eventually settled upon the English churchman and martyr Thomas Becket. And in 1879 Tennyson turned over to Irving a manuscript so large that, according to Bram Stoker, "it was for stage purposes much in the position of a block of Carrara marble from which the statue has to be patiently hewn."[1] What Tennyson had given Irving was a five-act behemoth, filled with historical pageantry, spectacle, and the grandeur of pseudo-Shakespearian verse. The play did not please everyone. The critic of the *Pall Mall Gazette* expressed the opinion: "Only idolatry could assert that 'Becket' was a delight to read, only hysteria could flutter itself into the belief that it gave any glory to the stage . . . . Lord Tennyson studied the Shakespearian drama to his bane. The result is a chilling parody; there is no throb of life in it."[2]Despite the reservations of the critics, Irving had faith in the play.[3] Suitably cut and altered by Irving (with Tennyson's approval), *Becket* was to be one of Irving's greatest successes.[4] Following its initial production in 1893 *Becket* remained in Irving's repertoire until his death in 1905. Becket was the last role Irving played; he died less than an hour after speaking the final lines of the play: "Into Thy hands, O Lord — into Thy hands!"[5]

The incidental music to *Becket* was composed by Charles Villiers Stanford (1852-1924), one of the major figures in later nineteenth- and early twentieth-century English music. The son of a Dublin lawyer and a prodigy both as a pianist and composer, Stanford received his university education at Cambridge, where he first served as organist at Trinity College and later

Kenneth DeLong is an Associate Professor in the Department of Music at the University of Calgary. Denis Salter is an Assistant Professor in the Department of Drama at the University of Calgary. This article forms part of an intended study of incidental music at the Lyceum Theatre during the tenure of Henry Irving.

(beginning in 1887) held the chair of Professor of Music. When the Royal College of Music opened in 1883, Stanford was invited to serve as professor of composition and conductor of the Royal College orchestra. Stanford held both his College and Cambridge posts concurrently until the end of his life. Intelligent, energetic, and somewhat irascible, Stanford rapidly emerged as a leader (together with Sir Hubert Parry) of what is known today as the modern renaissance of English music.[6] As a composer Stanford was astonishingly prolific, especially considering his many academic duties: his works include not only 31 oratorios, 7 symphonies, 19 large chamber works, but also 9 full-length operas, music to 7 stage plays, as well as over 160 solo songs, choral part-songs, and many items of church music.[7] Stanford was legendary for his facility at musical composition: according to Stanford's long-time student Thomas Dunhill, "Even the most complicated orchestral works were written straight into score, in ink, without previous preparation. . . . His thought flowed as rapidly as that of an ordinary mortal when writing a letter."[8] In his attitude and approach to composition Stanford was something of a paradox: on the one hand he was "intensely and passionately conservative in music as in politics," — a trait that led him to compose a large amount of quasi-Brahmsian instrumental music — and on the other he was attracted to musical pictorialism and responded vividly to verbal images.[9] The split in Stanford's musical personality was recognized by Bernard Shaw, who described Stanford's music as "a record of fearful conflict between the aboriginal Celt and the Professor."[10] Although in the bulk of his music the 'Professor' is clearly in ascendent, in his operas and, especially, in his incidental music to plays — works which depend for their success upon inspiration from extra-musical sources — the intensity of the 'aboriginal Celt' is much in evidence. Stanford was a thoroughgoing Victorian and, as Vaughan Williams has remarked, "his music is in the best sense of the word Victorian, that is to say it is the musical counterpart of the art of Tennyson, Watts and Matthew Arnold."[11]

Stanford had gotten to know Tennyson through the poet's sons, Hallam and Lionel, when they were undergraduates together at Cambridge; and over the years a warm friendship between Stanford and Tennyson had developed, a friendship that inspired Stanford to set many of Tennyson's poems to music.[12] It was Tennyson who in 1876 had asked Stanford to compose the music to *Queen Mary* — music which first brought Stanford to general public notice — and it was also Tennyson who, some seventeen years later, suggested to Henry Irving that Stanford be approached to provide music for *Becket*. In his autobiography, *Pages from an Unwritten Diary*, Stanford recalled in dialogue form the discussion that led to his writing the music for *Becket*:

> *I had a visit from genial Bram Stoker, his secretary, who told me that Irving had visited Lord Tennyson a short time before his death in 1892, had arranged to produce "Becket," and that Tennyson had expressed a wish that I should compose the music for it, to which suggestion Irving had warmly agreed.*

Bram Stoker. *"Will you undertake it?"*

C.V.S. *"Nothing would give me greater pleasure."*

B.S. *"Very well. The Chief dislikes talking business, so will you tell me what your terms will be?"*

C.V.S. *"No terms. It will be of the greatest interest to me to write it, and if only out of respect and affection for Lord Tennyson, I should not ask for anything."*

B.S. *"The Chief won't let you do that."*

C.V.S. *"He will, if you tell him what I say."*

B.S. *"He will not. I know him. You had better tell me what you think fair."*

C.V.S. *"If he must, he must. I don't know what to say: you know what he gives other people for such work."*

B.S. *"Would you accept (for performance right only of course) two hundred pounds?"*

C.V.S. *"It's a great deal too much."*

B.S. *"The Chief won't let you take less."*

C.V.S. *"He's an impossible man. Well, so be it."*

B.S. *"Then you are to come down and see him tomorrow morning, and he will go through the points of the play with you."*

*I go down to the Lyceum Theatre next day, and Irving shows me everything he wants. But at the end of the discussion,*

Irving. *"I am much obliged to you for agreeing to the terms Stoker suggested."*

C.V.S. *"They are a great deal too much."*

I. *"They are not; two hundred pounds was it? We'll make it three."*

C.V.S. *"You will not."*

I. *"Then you shan't write the music. I mean what I say."*

C.V.S. *"You're an impossible man!"* *(Exit.)*

*When the music was delivered, the cheque was for three, not two hundred, and for guineas not pounds. He gave me as many rehearsals as I wanted, and the whole atmosphere of the theatre from the leading actor down to the call-boy was one of consideration, thoroughness, and unruffled temper.*[13]

Stanford's incidental music to *Becket* was composed to enhance and underline a dramatic conception of the play that originally stemmed from Irving. In a letter to Hallam Tennyson, Irving explained that in his view " 'Becket' is a very noble play, with something of that lofty feeling and that far-reaching influence, which belong to a 'passion play.' "[14] Clearly, in adapting Tennyson's play for the stage, it had been Irving's decided intention to strengthen its resemblance to a passion play, for, as he once explained to an interviewer: "Tennyson's Becket seems to me to be resolute chiefly for martyrdom . . . ."[15] The development of character in Irving's stage version shows the various stages of spiritual growth by which the Archbishop eventually achieves the grandeur of martyrdom. In the early scenes — particularly in the second of the play's two prologues — he is chiefly a man of the world, a boon companion to King Henry. He later becomes Archbishop, and as a spiritual leader of the people in conflict with the usurping secular authority of the crown, he undergoes a period of trials and tribulations. In the conclusion to Irving's version of the drama, Becket achieves a state of transcendent grace when he is murdered by the "King's Men" and, in a sublime apotheosis, leaves his earthy existence behind and rises up into the arms of his Lord. Irving's interpretation of Becket's character and his studied arrangement of the plot as an unfolding spiritual journey were never in doubt: the cumulative impression, Laurence Irving reminds us, was of an "act of worship" in which the actor and his audience were spiritually united.[16]

## I

In composing the music to *Becket*, Stanford appears to have taken as his initial point of reference Mendelssohn's incidental music to Shakespeare's *A Midsummer Night's Dream*, music which Mendelssohn had completed in 1842 and that by the 1890s had already attained the status of a classic. Both scores are approximately the same length — about 200 pages of full orchestral score — and include an extended overture, shorter interludes between the acts (entr'actes), songs, as well as brass fanfares and several lengthy melodramas: music — over which the actors speak — that is designed to accompany and reinforce certain salient speeches.[17] Like Mendelssohn, Stanford's approach to the composition of incidental music is essentially pictorial and atmospheric. However, because of the marked difference between the two plays, the actual sound of the music is very different: Mendelssohn's score suggests the fairy realm of Oberon and Titania, whereas Stanford's music for *Becket*, grand and noble, frequently conveys the sense of impending tragedy — qualities appropriate to the pageantry and spectacle of the Lyceum production for which it was written. To evoke the specific 'historical' atmosphere of the play, Stanford employs as his principal musical idea the plainsong melody "Telluris ingens conditor," the actual vesper hymn that, according to tradition, was sung the very night the historical Becket was murdered.[18] This melody, a metaphor for Becket and inextricably associated with the Catholic Church and the Middle Ages, is woven into the musical tapestry and serves both as a point of local color and as a symbol for the martyred Becket. To provide a foil to the severity of the "Telluris" music and to strengthen the Medieval atmosphere of the score, Stanford also includes several short songs composed in the style of the troubadours.

The most musically significant portions of the score — the overture and the entr'actes — tend to anticipate rather than follow the story line and support the play by sympathetic juxtaposition rather than by direct involvement. Here again Stanford follows Mendelssohn's lead. In his treatise entitled *Musical Composition*, Stanford comments:

> *The principles which govern symphonic poems also apply to the incidental music to plays . . . . He [the composer] must not forget, however, that except where he writes an undercurrent accompani-*

> *ment for a scene where the action is proceeding (of which Mendelssohn's* Midsummer Night's Dream *is a wholly admirable example), he is, as a rule, anticipating action to come, rather than commenting on situations which are past. His overture and entr'actes, therefore, must be intelligible as absolute music, giving the atmosphere of the play rather than relying on realistic moments.*[19]

Following his own precepts, Stanford treats the overture and entr'acte music to *Becket* as short symphonic poems, through which he conveys in symphonic terms the mood and dramatic significance of each ensuing scene or act.

The other powerful influence on Stanford evident in his music for *Becket* is that of Wagner. Like many English musicians of his day, Stanford received the finishing touches to his musical education on the Continent; but unlike most of his contemporaries (men like Arthur Sullivan), Stanford retained a life-long interest in contemporary European music. In the 1870s when Stanford was studying in Germany, Wagner and Wagnerism, pro or con, was the issue of the day; and Stanford, always keen for anything new, was among the audience at the first production of Wagner's great operatic tetralogy, *The Ring of the Nibelung.*[20] Although usually associated with Brahms and musical conservatism, Stanford always remained a supporter of Wagner's music, even when he was repulsed by the fanatical fervor of his fans. Stanford admired Wagner the artist, the supreme man of the theatre, and he grasped the significance of Wagner's device of employing leitmotifs (leading motives) as a means to unify and give meaning to a long, complex drama. In his chapter on incidental music for plays, Stanford emphasizes that:

> *Even when the phrases are short, they should always be suggestive of some link with the musical design of the whole; "leading motives," in fact, on a small and well-defined scale.*[21]

Similar to Wagner's *The Flying Dutchman* or *Die Meistersinger*, Stanford unifies his musical score to *Becket* by the judicious use of selected key leitmotifs — in particular, the plainsong melody "Telluris ingens conditor" — which are subjected to various ingenious transformations. Thus in his music to *Becket,* Stanford walked a path that led between his two models: generally, the score follows the pattern established by Mendelssohn, that of concentrating on the pictorial and the descriptive elements in the drama; but far more than Mendelssohn, Stanford unifies his score through the use of leitmotifs. With these leitmotifs he provides his own interpretation of the play, an interpretation that brings into relief the "passion play" elements with which the script is filled.

This serious and somewhat intellectual approach to the composition of music for plays was, incidentally, rather different from that taken by most composers and arrangers of theatre music during this period. Most theatrical productions did contain an abundance of music, but it was usually of the hack variety and only roughly tailored to fit a specific play. As the critic of *The Saturday Review* pointed out:

> *The scant attention which the ordinary audience is accustomed to pay to the music played between the acts of the drama must make it a hard matter for a manager to resist the temptation to place the music of a new play entirely in the hands of one of those theatrical music-contractors who will supply you with as much or as little music as you choose. They have stores of ready-made melodrama fitted to every situation which playwright ever devised; there is no pride about them, you can take as little or as much as you like. . . . Their overtures . . . generally bear a striking family likeness to that old favourite,* Bauer und Dichter, *and their idea of the fitness of things induces them to usher in the last act of a tragedy by a rollicking waltz — presumably to keep up the spirits of the audience.*[22]

At this time it was common practice for musical directors to travel the land with a collection of suitable musical fragments, popularly called 'hurries,' 'slows,' 'agits' 'struggles,' 'hornpipes,' etc., that could be applied to any number of typical dramatic situations. With such a volume to hand, it was only a matter of a few hours to piece together the music needed for an entire evening's dramatic entertainment.[23] It was against this widespread, makeshift tradition that Henry Irving reacted when he took over the management of the Lyceum Theatre. For his major productions, often many years in gestation and costing vast sums, Irving commissioned the finest composers of the day to write the music:

> *Fortunately for the small minority who listen to the music when they go to the play, Mr. Irving — very greatly to his credit — has always at the Lyceum set his face against the rough-and-ready system which obtains at too many theatres. The artistic feeling which characterizes everything that he undertakes does not stop short at the footlights, but he is careful that — for those who choose to listen — ears as well as eyes shall have the best possible fare.*[24]

Through his attention to every detail of production and his efforts to incorporate all the arts into the service of the drama, Irving, like Wagner, created a theatre whose grandeur and spectacle have remained unsurpassed.[25]

## II

Broadly viewed, Stanford's incidental music to *Becket* consists of two functionally separate but thematically linked types: first, there is the music that accompanies and supports the dramatic action — fanfares, short interludes between scenes, songs, and melodramas; and second, there is the incidental music proper — that is, the overture and the entr'acte music. In quantity, the music heard during the progress of the play comprises approximately 30 percent of the total score. As the critic for *The Saturday Review* commented: "Professor Stanford has always remembered that 'the play's the thing,' and his music is always subordinated to the dramatic action."[26] Thus much of this music consists of either short brass fanfares to introduce King

Henry (Act III, Scene I) or short orchestral passages (circa 30 seconds in length) to cap a scene and to smooth the transition to the next one. The music intended to be played while the actors actually speak is limited almost entirely to a brief spot in the second scene of the prologue, where King Henry and Queen Eleanor converse, and to Act II and Act III, Scenes II and III — scenes set in or near Rosamund's bower. In these scenes the accent is upon the women in Henry's life — scenes which are treated as lyric interludes, separate from the central dramatic thrust.

The most extended scene with accompanying music — intended to serve as a vehicle for Irving's leading lady, Ellen Terry — comprises all of Act II and is entitled "Rosamund's Bower." To protect Rosamund de Clifford (his mistress) from the machinations of Queen Eleanor, Henry has hidden a restful bower at the center of a large, impenetrable labyrinth; it is this bower that forms the setting for all of Act II, the play's most picturesque and intimate portion. The musical entr'acte (also labelled "Rosamund's Bower") evokes the atmosphere of the bower and also the love of Henry and Rosamund. An "extremely delicate piece of work," the entr'acte "opens with a curious winding figure for the strings in unison, which is intended to represent the winding of the labyrinth."[27] This labyrinth idea is followed by a sensuous, lyric melody (the love theme), complete with harp and supported by amorous twitterings in the woodwinds, that is in turn followed by a central portion where the love theme is fully developed. In its pastoral evocation, this entr'acte rivals similar passages in Mendelssohn, Berlioz, and Wagner. The music of the entr'acte provides not only an appropriate atmospheric setting for the scene, but also the principal thematic ideas upon which the remainder of the music is based. At eight different points in this relatively brief act, and especially in places where the verbal imagery is vivid, fragments of the love theme steal in and out, each fragment appearing in distinctive orchestral and harmonic colors. At the conclusion of the act, as an accompaniment to Rosamund's wistful closing lines, "Rainbow, stay / Gleam upon gloom, / Bright as my dream, / Rainbow, stay!," there is an extended melodrama, including solo parts for two violins (representing the two lovers), that brings the act to a gentle, restful close (see Figures 2, 3, and 4). With its many pictorial and atmospheric elements, "Rosamund's Bower" is an example of the picturesque — in this instance made graphic and poignant through the subtlety and warmth of Stanford's music.

In contrast to the music just discussed, the incidental music itself (the overture and entr'actes) is not directly integrated into the dramatic action of the play and can be listened to and understood as independent pieces of music, albeit music with definite programmatic intent. A clear connection with the play is maintained, however, through a series of distinctive leitmotifs, intended to represent in musical terms particular persons and ideas; these leitmotifs are all heard, however briefly, at various points throughout the play. The purpose and function of the incidental music, beyond that of simple diversion during set changes, is to provide a musical commentary upon the principal issues developed in the play through a symphonic discussion of these leitmotifs — motifs imbued with both musical and extra-musical significance

Figure 2. Ellen Terry as Rosamund, in Act II, Rosamund's Bower. From the Souvenir Programme.

by their association with specific elements in the play. The incidental music thus moves beyond simple mood painting to a more serious level of dramatic interpretation: the portrayal of Becket as martyr.

Stanford employs two types of leitmotifs in his music to *Becket*. One type is the single remembrance motif which is repeated, essentially unvaried, to bring into sharper focus a certain character or emotion. The brusque, staccato chords which, according to *The Manchester Guardian*, "embody the danger that ever threatens Becket," are an example of this technique.[28] Dramatic, bold, and memorable, this motif, first heard at the opening of the overture, is effective in direct proportion to the restraint with which it is used. Aside from the overture, where it plays a significant role, this motif occurs only twice again in the entire score: once at the beginning of the final entr'acte, and again immediately prior to Becket's murder. The significance of the phrase, "King's men! King's men!," heard at several points throughout the play and shouted by Henry's fanatical followers just after they murder Becket, is brought to full meaning when placed in direct juxtaposition with this striking musical motif. The simplicity of the device is the key to its success.

The second type of leitmotif, more complex and sophisticated both in musical and dramatic terms, is, however, the more important. Here a musical idea, embodying the central issue of the drama, runs throughout the score as a thread and by its various transformations and combinations with other motives provides a musical commentary upon the action. It is a technique similar to that employed by Wagner in *Die Meistersinger*, where the "Preislied" — the song with which Walter wins the singing contest and his bride, Eva, — informs the entire opera.[29] Although present in fragmentary form throughout, only in the final act of the opera, at the maturity of the dramatic action, is the "Preislied" presented in full. Similarly, in his music to *Becket*, Stanford uses the plainsong melody "Telluris ingens conditor" as his principal leitmotif; and by tracing its transformation throughout the score, the listener can follow Stanford's conception of the drama as a form of "passion play."

The "Telluris" theme is, of course, Becket himself, and consequently the overture is centered around this important theme. But Stanford does not write a conventional overture along the lines of Weber or Rossini. Rather he uses the overture as a way to convey musically the initial stages of Becket's growth from man-of-the-world to triumphant churchman. Thus unlike most overtures to theatrical productions and even most operas, Stanford's overture is only concerned with a few central thematic ideas and does not try to tell the story in brief. On the simplest level the overture, "agitated and stormy,"[30] evokes the turbulence and stress which characterize the play and Becket's life. The introduction opens with the bold chords previously mentioned, interweaving with them fragments of the "Telluris" melody, here treated as a musical embryo. Following a short period of musical "groping," the music becomes more agitated and accelerates into the main body of the overture, a stormy D minor allegro. The main body of the overture preserves the outline of a typical Romantic sonata-form movement, including the expected exposition of themes, their development, and their re-statement. But combined with and

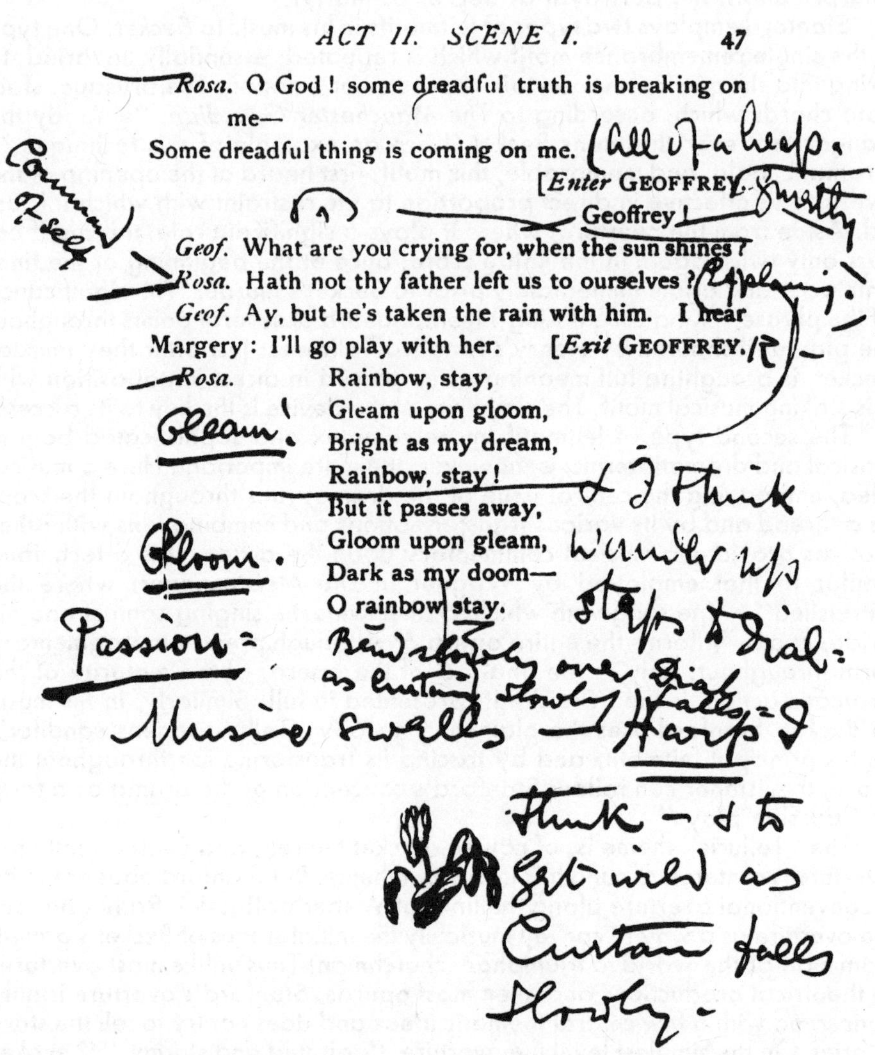

ACT II. SCENE I. 47

*Rosa.* O God! some dreadful truth is breaking on me—
Some dreadful thing is coming on me.
[*Enter* GEOFFREY.
Geoffrey!
*Geof.* What are you crying for, when the sun shines?
*Rosa.* Hath not thy father left us to ourselves?
*Geof.* Ay, but he's taken the rain with him. I hear Margery: I'll go play with her. [*Exit* GEOFFREY.
*Rosa.* Rainbow, stay,
Gleam upon gloom,
Bright as my dream,
Rainbow, stay!
But it passes away,
Gloom upon gleam,
Dark as my doom—
O rainbow stay.

Figure 3. Ellen Terry's study-book, for Act II, Rosamund's Bower. Courtesy the Folger Shakespeare Library.

integrated into this structure, and gradually growing to dominate it, is the "Telluris" melody associated with Becket. Initially, only the first phrase of the plainsong is heard; but as the overture proceeds, phrase is joined to phrase until the entire chant-melody is heard. The coda, grand and imposing, is a peroration on the "Telluris" theme, now presented with full organ to augment the strings, woodwinds, and brass. The overture thus depicts the gradual spiritual development of Becket from the opening of the play, where he is a friend and companion to the King, to the end of Act I, the point at which Becket embraces his destiny as Archbishop and defies the King by his refusal to relinquish the authority of the church over its bishops. The coda of the overture is recalled twice during the final scene of Act I: once when Becket is himself defied by the Archbishop of York, a supporter of the King (see Figure 1); and again at the very end of the act when Becket is hailed by the people with the words: "Blessed is he that cometh in the name of the Lord!" In these two instances the music of the coda is treated in the same way as the opening chords — as a local, referential theme to underline a point of stage action. And although the "Telluris" theme is used several more times in the score, it is never again encountered in this specific orchestral setting. Aside from a few brief, fragmentary references, the complete "Telluris" theme only occurs twice more in the play, both times in climactic scenes where Becket asserts the authority of the church over the state. The first occurrence is during the "Meeting of the Kings" scene at Montmirail (Act III, Scene I), where Louis of France makes an abortive attempt to reconcile Becket and Henry; the final occurrence is during the last scene of the play when it is sung by monks as the events leading to Becket's martyrdom move inexorably forward. The intoning during this final scene of the "Telluris" melody, now heavy with the weight of cumulative associations, gives the martyrdom scene a special poignancy and force.

Together with the "Telluris" theme, Stanford in his music to *Becket* employs a second principal leitmotif, nearly equal in importance to the "Telluris" melody itself. This second leitmotif, introduced as a small point of stage business in the second scene of the prologue, consists of a sad, plaintive folksong sung by Eleanor — Henry's once loved but now abandoned queen. The words are as follows:

*Over! the sweet summer closes,*
*And never a flower at the close;*
*Over and gone with the roses,*
*Not over and gone with the rose.*

The final phrase, "Not over and gone with the rose," is a reference to Henry's latest love: Rosamund de Clifford, Eleanor's rival. This leitmotif, presented simply and without fanfare, is associated throughout the play with Queen Eleanor and the impermanence of human relationships — not only the relationship between Eleanor and Henry but also, by implication, the relationship between Henry and Becket, once the closest of friends. Aside from the prologue, this motif recurs at the conclusion of the first entr'acte (entitled "King Henry"), where together with a fragment of the "Telluris"

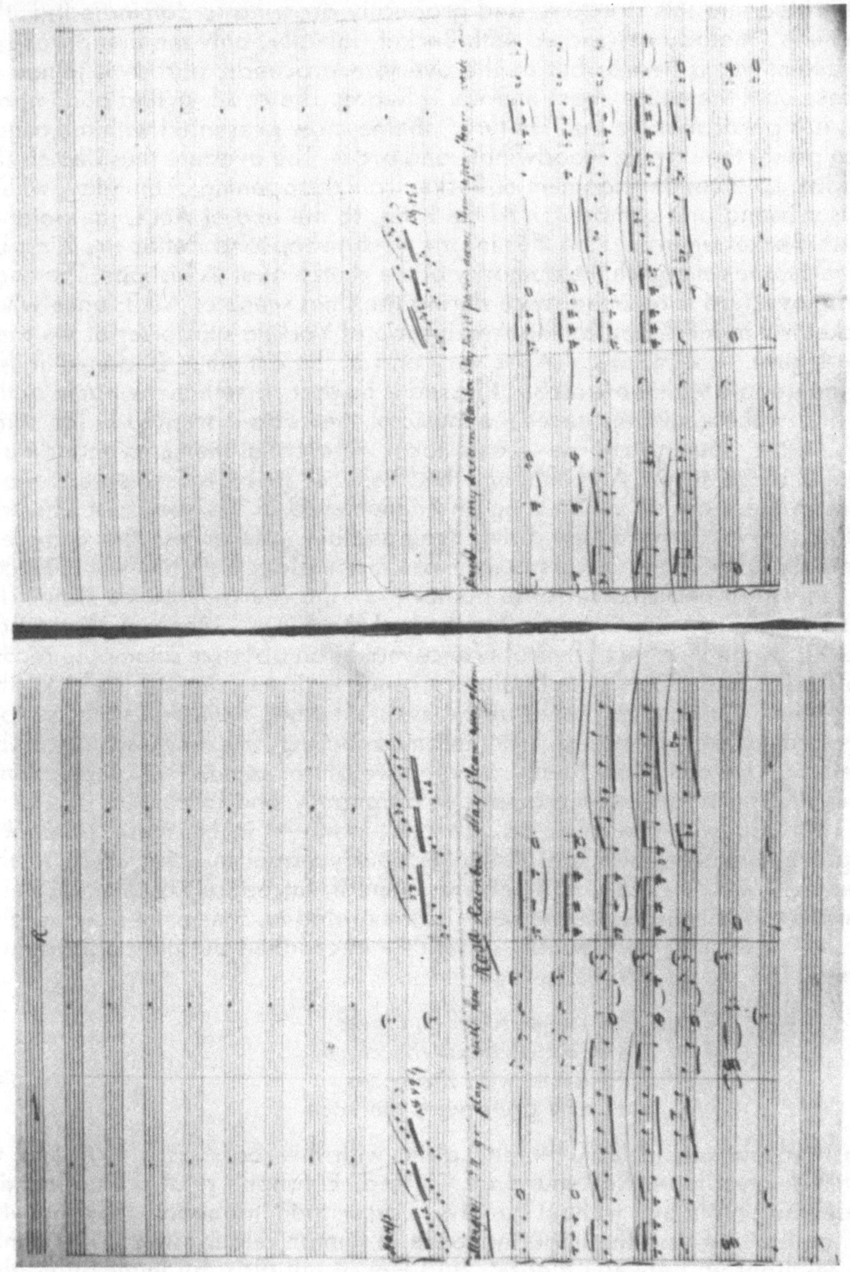

Figure 4. Stanford's score for *Becket*: Rosamund's song at the conclusion of Act II, Rosamund's Bower. Courtesy the Royal College of Music.

theme it forms a reflective coda to an otherwise vigorous and energetic movement. Presented here in this way, these motifs musically convey to the audience the King's principal concerns (his difficulties with Becket and Eleanor) without explicit verbal statement — a classic instance of Wagnerian procedure. The full significance of this theme is only made manifest, however, when transformed it becomes the central melodic idea for the last entr'acte — Becket's funeral march.

This entr'acte, entitled "The Martyrdom," is musically the most important portion of the score. Here Stanford gathers his principal leitmotifs and transforms them into a grand and sublime funeral march for the martyred Archbishop. Henry Irving told Stanford that "He never missed coming down behind the curtain to hear the last *entr'acte* (the funeral march);" and it was also the music played at Stanford's own funeral in 1924.[31] It is music for the death of a hero. The funeral march opens with the same chords that were heard at the beginning of the overture, chords which now signal that the end is near. The march proper, a lament, centers upon a melody, dark, sombre, and modal, that is a transformation of Eleanor's song, "Over! the sweet summer closes." The second portion of this melody, more intense, grows organically out of the first and at its high point incorporates a motive from the third entr'acte entitled "Becket's Rest." Following the opening march section, the gloomy key of D minor gives way to a gentle, yielding trio section in D major. Here smooth string figures and harp provide background support for fragments in the woodwinds of the "Telluris" melody: the martyred Becket is now in heaven. The second portion of the trio consists of a grand climax, complete with brass and percussion, that forms a further transformation of Becket's lament: Becket is transfigured. Following a repeat of these two expansive phrases of music, the march returns, "handsome and pathetic,'[32] only this time it is accompanied by anguished, chromatic string figures. In terms of stage reality, the awful trial has yet to take place. Psychologically, Stanford's entr'acte leads the audience away from the time-bound events of the stage to a contemplation of their significance: a contemplation expressed in symphonic terms and given added meaning through the fresh combination and transformation of the central leitmotifs heard throughout the play. At the end of the entr'acte, Stanford returns the audience to the here and now — the north transept of Canterbury Cathedral on the evening of Tuesday, 29 December 1170 — and to the enactment of the final, cathartic scene (see Figure 5).

## III

Taken as a whole, the overture and four entr'actes can be viewed as a five-movement programmatic symphony based upon themes from the play. The overture serves as the first movement, setting the general tone and mood; "King Henry," the first entr-acte, is the lively scherzo; "Rosamund's Bower," the second entr'acte, provides a picturesque interlude (much like "Le Ball" from Berlioz's *Symphonie Fantastique*); "Becket's Rest," the third entr'acte, forms the lyric slow movement; and "The Martyrdom," the fourth and final entr'acte, provides a finale in the form of a grand apotheosis. As Wagner

Figure 5. North Transept of Canterbury Cathedral. Act IV, Scene iii. By William Telbin. From the Souvenir Programme.

in *Die Götterdämmerung* provides the slain Siegfried with a musical funeral oration that sums up his deeds and accomplishments, so Stanford provides the martyred Becket with his funeral oration, revealing his reward in the world to come and expressing the glory of his martyrdom.

Through the symphonic organization of the overture and the entr'actes, Stanford infuses his incidental music to *Becket* with an interpretative dimension and significance not often encountered in earlier instances of theatre music. With his attention both to he details of the stage action and to the broader considerations of the drama, Stanford's music to *Becket* represents one of the finest examples of Victorian theatre music — one in which the composer joins with the actors, director, and designers to create a unified interpretation of the drama. The masterly evocation of mood, the symphonic breadth of the entr'actes, the adroit handling of the leitmotifs, and the effective, if unobtrusive, support of the action — all contribute to make *Becket* "a happy alliance between the musical and dramatic arts."[33] Even Bernard Shaw, normally no great fan of English music, remarked:

> *Technically, it is a very good piece of work — it has qualities that may almost be described as moral excellences. For instance, the handling of the orchestra is first rate: by which I do not mean,*

> *if you please, that there are sensational* tremolandos, *or voluptuous murmurs for the wind, or delicate embroideries for the flute, or solos for the English horn, or scintillations for the triangle, or, generally speaking, any of that rouging of the cheeks of the music and underlining of its eyes which is so cheap nowadays: I mean that the composer knows how and where to get his tone of the right shade and of the best quality, how to balance it, how to vary it otherwise than by crudely obvious contrast and how to get from the full band that clear, smooth, solid effect for which one has to go to Brahms, or even back to Cherubini, for satisfactory examples.*
>
> *Add to this a complete intellectual mastery of harmony, and you have an equipment which enables the composer to do anything he wants to do within the known limits of musical composition.*[34]

*Becket* was one of Irving's greatest roles and a fine example of his 'saintly' style. According to Stanford:

> *Irving thought "Becket" the finest tragedy since "King John." . . . So imbued was he with the spirit of the play, that an actor-friend of mine who went to see him after a performance and found him sitting in his room in the Archbishop's dress . . . was dismissed (quite genuinely) with a "God bless you" and an uplifted hand accompanying an Episcopal benediction.*[35]

And Naomi Jacob, commenting to her mother about the disappointing everyday demeanor of certain church dignitaries received the following response: "Yes . . . . You see, you saw Irving as Becket—."[36] The Victorian theatre of spectacle, where all the arts were pressed into the service of a central dramatic idea, has passed, replaced today, perhaps, by such movies as *The Ten Commandments*, *A Man for All Seasons*, or *Gandhi*. But in music such as that composed by Stanford for Tennyson's *Becket*, one may yet catch a glimpse of the grandeur that attended Irving and the Lyceum.

## NOTES

[1]Bram Stoker, *Personal Reminiscences of Henry Irving* (London: William Heinemann, 1906), I, [209].

[2]*Pall Mall Gazette*, 7 February 1893. This review, unusually perceptive, was probably written by the lecturer and journalist Rev. Hugh R. Haweis, who wrote music criticism, beginning in 1884, for the *Pall Mall Gazette*. Evidently, he had read Tennyson's original play, for throughout the review he compares it to Irving's stage adaptation. He was not happy with either. See Christopher Kent, "Periodical Critics of Drama, Music, and Art, 1830-1914: A Preliminary List," *Victorian Periodicals Reviews*, 13 (1980), 41.

[3]See, for example, Frederick Wedmore in the *Academy*, 18 February 1893; W. Moy Thomas in the *Graphic*, 11 February 1893; and the *Spectator*, 25 February 1893.

[4]Stoker, *Personal Reminiscences of Henry Irving*, I, 224-25.

[5]Alfred Lord Tennyson, *Becket*: As Arranged for the Stage by Henry Irving ([London: n.p.,

1893]), p. 70. All further references to and quotations from the play come from this edition. Regrettably, we have not been able to locate Irving's promptbook.

[6]The principal biographical sources for Stanford include: "Charles Villiers Stanford," *The Musical Times*, 39 (1898), 785-93; John F. Porte, *Sir Charles V. Stanford* (London: Kegan Paul, 1921); Thomas F. Dunhill, "C. V. Stanford: some aspects of his work and influence," *Proceedings of the Royal Musical Association*, 53 (1927), 41-65; H. Plunket Greene, *Charles Villiers Stanford* (London: Edward Arnold, 1935); J. A. Fuller-Maitland, *The Music of Parry and Stanford* (Cambridge: W. Heffer and Sons, 1934); and Frederick Hudson, "Stanford, Charles Villiers," in *The New Grove Dictionary of Music and Musicians*, 1980, Vol. 18, pp. 70-74. To these secondary sources must be added Stanford's three books of articles and personal memoirs: *Studies and Memories* (London: Edward Arnold, 1908); *Pages from an Unwritten Diary* (London: Edward Arnold, 1914); and *Interludes, Records and Reflections* (London: John Murray, 1922).

[7]A catalogue of works, gathering and correcting information from previous catalogues, can be found in Frederick Hudson, "A Catalogue of the Works of Charles Villiers Stanford (1852-1924)," *Music Review*, 25 (1964), 44-57.

[8]Dunhill, "C. V. Stanford," p. 45.

[9]Edgar L. Bainton in "Charles Villiers Stanford by Some of his Pupils," *Music and Letters*, 5 (1924), 201.

[10]Bernard Shaw, *Shaw's Music*, ed. Dan H. Laurence (London: Max Reinhardt, 1981), II, 879.

[11]R. Vaughan Williams in "Charles Villiers Stanford by Some of his Pupils," p. 195.

[12]H. Plunket Greene, *Charles Villiers Stanford*, pp. 246-49, chronicles the details of Stanford's long friendship with Tennyson, citing several letters and humorous anecdotes. On the death of Tennyson in 1892, Stanford contributed an affectionate *in memoriam* article to the *Cambridge Review*, 15 October 1892 (reprinted in *Studies and Memories*, pp. 89-98). See also Stanford's *Pages from an Unwritten Diary*, pp. 228-33, and "Charles Villiers Stanford," *The Musical Times*, 39 (1898), 792-93. The list of Tennyson's poems set to music by Stanford is long and includes his ballad "The Revenge" (long popular with amateur choral societies), "The Voyage of Maeldune," the ode "Carmen Saeculare," written to commemorate Queen Victoria's 1887 jubilee, as well as many shorter poems that serve as the texts to Stanford's songs.

[13]Stanford, *Pages from an Unwritten Diary*, pp. 230-31. Bram Stoker, however, states that Irving and Tennyson each had separately arrived at the conclusion that Stanford should be approached to write the music for *Becket*:

". . . when I asked Tennyson what composer he would wish to do the music for his play he said: "Villiers Stanford!" He and Irving had independently chosen the same man. How this belief was justified is known to all who have heard the fine *Becket* music." Stoker, *Personal Reminiscences of Henry Irving*, I, 232. See also p. 223. A lengthy article by G. B. Burgin in *The Idler*, 3 (March 1893), [122] -41 describes in detail the rehearsals for *Becket*, including the manner in which the music was integrated with the play.

[14][Hallam Tennyson], *Alfred Lord Tennyson: A Memoir By His Son* (London: Macmillan and Co., *1897), II, 196.*

[15]T. H., "Mr. Irving's Ecclesiastical Characters: A Midnight Chat on the Stage of the Lyceum," *St. Paul's*, 1 (March 1894), 7.

[16]Laurence Irving, *Henry Irving: The Actor and His World* (London: Faber and Faber, 1951), p. 560.

[17]We should like to thank the Royal College of Music, London, and its deputy reference librarian, Joan Littlejohn, for their assistance in making available to us a microfilm of the unpublished score (RCM MS 4248) of Stanford's incidental music to *Becket*.

[18]Three different versions of the "Telluris ingens conditor" are cited in John R. Bryden and David G. Hughes, comp., *An Index of Gregorian Chant* (Cambridge: Harvard University Press, 1969), I, 413. Stanford used a slight variant of the version found the *Antiphonale Monasticum* (Tournai: Desclée and Co., 1934), p. 142. Stanford's extensive knowledge of modal theory was acquired through a systematic course of instruction with the organist and theorist W. S. Rockstro, a course Stanford undertook to prepare himself for the composition of Robert Bridges' "Eden" in 1891. Although he was a poet, Bridges had a solid grounding in sixteenth-century music and suggested to Stanford that the preliminary "Heaven" section of the oratorio be composed in a modal, sixteenth-century style, a suggestion Stanford followed. The *Becket* music,

composed shortly after "Eden," also contains many modal elements, used to evoke the Medieval atmosphere of *Becket*. See Stanford, *Pages from an Unwritten Diary*, pp. 273-75.

[19]C. V. Stanford, *Musical Composition* (London: Macmillan and Co., 1911), p. 161.

[20]Stanford's support of Wagner at this period (1875-95) was unfashionable in England. In response to a particularly virulent attack on Wagner, Stanford wrote an article, "Defence of Richard Wagner: reply to Rowbotham," *Nineteenth Century*, 24 (1888), 727 ff., in which he defended Wagner. (The article is reprinted in Stanford, *Studies and Memories*, pp. 31-42.) The English fascination with Wagner, initiated by Bernard Shaw, *The Perfect Wagnerite* (London, 1898), and Ernest Newman, *Study of Wagner* (London, 1899) and *Wagner as Man and Artist* (London, 1914), is of a later date.

[21]Stanford, *Musical Composition*, p. 162.

[22]*The Saturday Review*, 4 March 1893.

[23]The somewhat scanty literature on nineteenth-century theatre music includes: Norman O'Neill, "Music to Stage Plays," *Proceedings of the Royal Musical Association*, 37 (1911), 85-102; David Mayer, "Nineteenth Century Theatre Music," *Theatre Notebook*, 30 (1976), 115-22; and David Mayer, "The Music of Melodrama," in David Bradby, Louis James, and Bernard Sharratt, eds., *Performance and Politics in Popular Drama* (Cambridge, 1980), pp. 49-63. A recent edition of *The Bells*, edited by David Mayer (Manchester, 1980) contains a piano reduction of the musical score composed by Etienne Singla; and a recording of *The Bells*, complete with music and with Eric Jones-Evans in the central role of Mathias, is available on cassette tape from the University of Bristol.

[24]*The Saturday Review*, 4 March 1893.

[25]William Wallace, "Sir Henry Irving's Claims," *National Review*, 28 (1896), 76, described the atmosphere of the Lyceum Theatre during this period as follows:

> *There is an air about a Lyceum audience like nothing else in the world. Each face is the face of a fervid worshipper who looks upon the rising of the curtain as the rending of a veil which will reveal a great mystery. As* Parsifal *at Bayreuth seals for hours afterwards the lips of those who have beheld The Vision of the Grail, so also does a play at the Lyceum touch with some vague mysticism the minds of those who have formed the audience, giving them a dim sense of having taken part in some sacred function.*

See also Michael R. Booth, *Victorian Spectacular Theatre 1850-1910* (London: Routledge & Kegan Paul, 1981).

[26]*The Saturday Review*, 4 March 1893. Other descriptive reviews of the music to *Becket* include: *Pall Mall Gazette*, 7 February 1893; *The Daily News* 8 February 1893; *The Evening News and Post*, 7 February 1893; *The Stage*, 9 February 1893; *The Manchester Guardian*, 7 February 1893; and *The Musical Times*, 34 (1893), 151.

[27]*The Saturday Review*, 4 March 1893.

[28]*The Manchester Guardian*, 7 February 1893.

[29]According to L. H. Heward, "Charles Villiers Stanford by Some of his Pupils," p. 203, Stanford's "favourite operas were *Meistersinger* and *Othello*." And in his memoirs, written shortly before his death, Stanford commented as follows about the use of leitmotifs in Wagner, particularly in *The Ring of the Nibelung*:

> *The theory of* leit-motives *was, to my mind, carried too far, even to annoyance. The motives were so interwoven that they were often of no avail. Less of them would have effected more, and would have heightened their value. As it is, the plethora of over-done phrases of similitude, so valuable in themselves when used with economy, is threatening to destroy what is inherent in opera and which, properly used, is essential to characterisation and to situation . . . . In lesser quantities, as Wagner used them in the "Dutchman," and even in the "Meistersinger," they carry a fuller conviction to the hearer. (Stanford, Interludes,* p. 145.)

[30]*The Musical Times*, 34 (1893), 151.

[31]The "Funeral March" from *Becket* was the only item from the score to be published; it has remained in the Stainer and Bell catalogue (Stanford's publishers) as a separate work and has recently received a new recording by Sir Adrian Boult and the London Symphony Orchestra (Lyrita, FRCS 71). H. Plunket Greene, *Charles Villiers Stanford*, p. 248.

[32] *Pall Mall Gazette,* 7 February 1893.
[33] *The Saturday Review,* 4 March 1893.
[34] Shaw, *Shaw's Music,* III, 174.
[35] Stanford, *Pages from an Unwritten Diary,* p. 231.
[36] Naomi Jacob, "Irving as Thomas Becket," in H. A. Saintsbury and Cecil palmer, eds., *We Saw Him Act* (1939; rpt. New York: Benjamin Blom, Inc., 1969), p. 323.

# Christopher Sly on the Stage

ELLEN DOWLING

Critics of Shakespeare's *The Taming of the Shrew* have long been fascinated with Christopher Sly — "by birth a pedlar, by education a card-maker, by transmutation a bear-herd," and, by his creator's artistry, a minor comic masterpiece.[1] Many have discoursed at great length on Sly's reason for being, establishing thematic links between the Sly story and the *Shrew* story, and pointing out parallels between the tinker who becomes a lord and the shrew who becomes a lady. For these scholars, the question is what to *make* of Sly and his retinue.[2] Directors and producers of the play, on the other hand, have long pondered the question of what to *do* with the "Presenters," and in the theatre, where scholarly debate must lead eventually to practical decision-making, the first choice any director of *Shrew* must make is whether or not to cut the Induction. For most directors, it is not a simple decision.

The early stage history of *The Taming of the Shrew* offers scanty information to a director seeking precedents for cutting or keeping the Induction. Christopher Sly and company appear in both the 1596 quarto edition of *The Taming of a Shrew* and the 1623 folio edition of *The Taming of the Shrew* — more or less: more in *A Shrew*, where the drunken tinker is given several opportunities to interrupt the action of the play he is watching, and where, at the end, he awakens to find himself once more in a field outside an alehouse, discusses with the Tapster ("Hostess" in *The Shrew*) the strange dream he has had, and leaves the stage determined to try out Ferrando's (Petruchio's) taming methods on his own wife back home; and less in *The Shrew* where Sly is heard from no more after Act I, scene 1, line 231. So we can assume that audiences then were entertained by Sly in one form or another, as they most likely were again in 1633 when "The Taminge of the Shrew" was "revived" at St. James's for the King and Queen. But thirty-four years later Sly had disappeared from the stage. In 1667, Samuel Pepys saw a production *Sauny the Scot: or, The Taming of the Shrew*, an adaptation of *A Shrew* by John Lacy, a member of the King's Company.[3] Lacy cut the Induction and re-arranged the plot to make "Sauny" (from "Sander," Grumio's counterpart in *A Shrew*) the main character. Sly was briefly resurrected in 1716, when two rival playwrights, Charles Johnson and Christopher Bullock, wrote their versions of the Sly story, both entitled *The Cobler of Preston*, but he was buried once again in the mid-eighteenth century when David Garrick produced his enormously popular *Catherine and Petruchio*.[4] It was not until 1844, nearly 100 years later, when Benjamin Webster decided to produce the Folio version of *The Taming of the Shrew*, Induction

Ellen Dowling is Assistant Professor of English at Texas A & M University.

and all, that Sly was restored to his original place in the theatre and his permanent place in Shakespearean criticism.

Since that time, most professional directors and producers (75% of them, in over sixty-five productions staged in the U.S. and Europe from 1844 to 1978) have chosen not to cut the tinker and his play-acting confederates. Significantly, when directors or producers have chosen to cut Sly, they usually feel obligated to explain their decision. In an interview published in *The New York Times* after the opening of their highly controversial, rough-and-tumble version of a Sly-less *Shrew* in 1905, Julia Marlowe and E. H. Sothern defended their decision to cut Sly by resting their case on the textual authority of "Fleay, Furnivall, and Furness," claiming that "it is the only indubitably spurious portion of the Text" and "has nothing to do with the play proper."[5] Others have cut the Induction "for purposes of expediencey"[6] (as Brooks Atkinson assumed in his review of Richard Boleslavsky's 1925 production at the Klaw Theatre, New York City), or in deference to their audiences: R.O. Ceballos, director of the 1978 Shakespeare Festival of Cincinnati, claimed in a program note that "Since it's become standard to drop the Sly scenes, most of the audience — not familiar with the text — would have questioned whether they were watching Shakespeare."[7] On the contrary, more likely most of them — at least the experienced playgoers — would have wondered, "What happened to Christopher Sly?"

The most important questions that need to be raised at this point are: 1) Why do so many directors choose to keep Sly (when cutting him would seem to be the easier choice — fewer actors to cast, fewer lines to work on, less scenery, less complicated staging); and 2) what theatrical effect does his presence have on the style of the play as a whole?

One practical reason why so many directors choose to keep the Induction is that it allows them to simplify the physical setting of the play. Once the basic set — the Lord's house — has been contructed, the subsequent scene changes can be facilitated by the Players themselves, who may carry their own props and furniture on to the stage, set up a drop cloth or curtain from which to make their entrances, and hang placards indicating "A Street in Padua," and so on. A simplified set design like this is not only economical but it also eliminates the kind of scenic clutter to which most nineteenth century theatres were (and some twentieth century theatres are) addicted. J. R. Planché, the designer who first suggested to Benjamin Webster that he replace Garrick's *Catherine and Petruchio* with Shakespeare's original play, believed that this simplicity of style was the concept's chief attraction.[8] Not all nineteenth century critics were ready for this innovation in stage design — the *Athenaeum* reviewer dismissed the whole idea as "pedantic affectation of accuracy"[9] — but most agreed with *The London Times* reviewer who praised the production, calling it "one of the most remarkable instances of modern theatre," and stressing that the staging "tended to give closeness to the action, and by constantly allowing a great deal of stage room, afforded a sort of freedom to all parties engaged."[10]

Yet the play can also be performed without the Induction — as it was by the American Conservatory Theatre company in 1973 — and still retain the ambiance of a *commedia dell'arte* romp put on by a band of wandering players atop wagon-stages, so one must not conclude that the presence of Sly and company is a prerequisite for simplified staging. What *is* necessary, most directors who keep the Induction believe, is the theatrical distancing effect which Sly's presence has on the audience. In the theatre, as Larry S. Champion has pointed out, the Induction "serves constantly to draw the filter of fiction before us lest we be tempted to forget that Kate is a purely artificial figure of farce and, like many an armchair critic, to become indignant that Shakespeare could consider such cruel mistreatment of womankind as comic. . . ."[11] With this idea in mind, Max Reinhardt chose to retain the Induction in his 1909 productin at the Deutsches Theater, Berlin, believing that this alone "would excuse Petruchio's intolerable behavior."[12] And Tyrone Guthrie, in both his 1939 production for the Old Vic and his 1954 production at Stratford, Ontario, chose to do likewise, claiming that the play, "without the framework, loses its best reason for being."[13]

Reviewers have generally concurred favorably with the director's choice to play it all to Sly. *The London Times* reviewer who saw Martin Harvey's 1913 production at the Prince of Wales Theatre felt that Sly's presence enabled the audience to relax: "It left us free to enjoy this 'pleasant conceited historie' as a piece of hearty fun, without bothering about its ethics or calculating its probability of its likeness to life."[14] As modern sensibilities about women's rights were raising the consciousnesses of most would-be admirers of Petruchio, a reviewer of Harcourt Williams' 1931 production at Sadler's Wells could claim, with some relief, that "the taming of poor Kate, which commonly grates harshly upon our polite ears, suddenly acquires the curious grace which belongs even to the roughest horse-play in a novel of Boccaccio."[15] Richard David, reviewing George Devine's 1954 production at Stratford-upon-Avon likewise felt that the double artifice made "palatable" the "creaky humor" of the play proper, and enabled modern audiences to endure those scenes "which are too roughly Elizabethan for our tastes."[16]

With Sly there to "soften the blow," the bounds of farce can be pushed to their furthest limits. If, as a reviewer of Ben Iden Payne's 1940 production at Stratford-upon-Avon claimed, the Induction enables the director to keep the comedy "on the plane of a drunken tinker's hallucination,"[17] then, as the reviewer of John Burrell's 1947 production at the Lyceum Theatre concluded, "hardly anything in it can be too theatrical,"[18] and, as in Trevor Nunn's 1967 production for the Royal Shakespeare Company, "the players can give performances in a riper, broader style than would otherwise be permissible."[19] Sly's presence thus has a two-fold effect on both the play and the audience, as Peter D. Smith, reviewer of Michael Langham's 1962 Stratford, Ontario production has noted: "On the one hand this episode in the fairy-tale of the battle of the sexes is removed one stage further from reality and its extravagance is accordingly made more acceptable; and, on the other, the audience, paradoxically, is given a keener sense of participation as these happily become involved in Sly's own enthusiasm."[20]

Once a director has decided to keep the Induction, he or she must then make several more important decisions, the first being to decide what is to happen to Sly and the others after I.i. According to the Folio, after Sly's last "enthusiastic" interjection (" 'Tis a very excellent piece of work, Madam lady. Would 'twere done") the stage direction reads, "They sit and mark." Does this mean that they unobtrusively watch the rest of the play until the audience forgets all about them, or is Sly expected to extemporize throughout, playing off the actors playing to him?

Some directors have chosen to simplify the problem by removing Sly all together after I.i., a solution first advanced by Samuel Phelps in his 1856 production at Sadler's Wells. Phelps himself played the drunken tinker and received accolades from reviewers who thought his performance, though of so brief a duration, outshone that of all the other actors, including Mr. Marston and Miss Atkinson, who played Petruchio and Kate. The reviewer from *The Examiner* found Sly's disappearance after I.i. thematically logical and dramtically effective, given the lushness of Phelp's performance and his emphasis on the tinker's overwhelming dim-wittedness, and asserted that "The stupidity of Sly causes his disappearance from the stage in the most natural way after the play itself has warmed into full action. He has of course no fancy for it, is unable to follow it, stares at it, and falls asleep over it. The sport of imagination acts upon him as a sleeping-draught, and at the end of the first act he is so fast asleep that it becomes matter of course to carry him away."[21] Augustin Daly repeated this procedure in his highly successful 1887 production in New York and 1888 production in London. William Gilbert's Sly was, understandably, so overshadowed by Ada Rehan's Kate and John Drew's Petruchio that the *Athenaeum* reviewer felt justified in claiming that the sleeping Sly's removal at the end of I.i. was "quite defensible. Shakespeare after the play is once launched ceases to concern himself with the bemused tinker. Why should not others follow his example?"[22] On the other hand, Andrew Leigh, playing Sly in Henry Cass's 1935 Old Vic production, gave such a masterful comic performance that *The London Times* reviewer was moved to praise the Induction as "a gleam of farce that shines on human vanity and exhibits in penetrating light the cruelty of farce itself" and to lament that "too soon poor Christopher gives sign of falling asleep and the taming itself takes the stage from him."[23] In spite of these notable exceptions, the decision to close the curtains on a sleeping Sly is rarely made in the theatre, a fact that may attest to Sir Arthur Quiller-Couch's feeling that something about this choice just doesn't seem right: "After all," he has said, "it is not the way of authors to invite public attention so subtly to the dullness or insipidity of their own compositions."[24]

A more practical disadvantage of this choice is that it wastes acting talent. As J. Dover Wilson has pointed out, "To keep three players up on the gallery throughout the play, speaking only occasionally and never able to help out the main action by doubling, would have seemed a crime to any practical stage manager of the period, unless he were very rich in actors."[25] To circumvent this "crime," some directors have experimented with a wide range of doubling possibilities, including the interesting procedure of doubling Sly and Petruchio. Oscar Asche tried this first in 1904, rather unsuccessfully, in Robert Atkins' opinion, since this caused "an act-long wait between the Induction and the play itself, which made nonsense of the close attachment of the one to the other."[26] Fritz Leiber played both Sly and Petruchio in a Chicago Civic Shakespeare Society production in 1930, and, more recently, Jonathan Pryce doubled a boorish, scenery-wrecking Sly with a leather-coated, motorcycle riding Petruchio in Michael Bogdanov's 1978 production for the Royal Shakespeare Company. (Reviewers of this production seem to agree with Mel Gussow of *The New York Times* that this concept had little thematic or structural relevance to the play, but that it encapsulated wonderfully the "outrageous anything-goes attitude of the director."[27]) The logistics of changing Sly into Petruchio and back again to Sly are, as can be imagined, rather complicated, since Petruchio is supposed to step on stage immediately after Sly's last interpolation at the end of I.i., and has only two lines of dialogue between Lucentio and Hortensio at the end of the play during which, if the director so desires, to change back into Sly.[28]

A more popular — and less problem-ridden — choice is to double the Presenters with characters who appear later in the play proper: the actor who plays the Lord, for example, could easily be doubled as Vincentio, his servants could become Petruchio's servants, Sly's "wife" could appear again as the Tailor or the Widow or Biondello — there are many possibilities. Sly could be pressed into service as the Pedant, as he was in Claude Gurney's 1937 New Theatre production and in the Young Vic's 1974 production, or the actor playing Sly could double as Petruchio's horse, as he did in Margaret Webster's 1951 production at the New York City Center, and in George Devine's 1953 and 1954 productions at Stratford-upon-Avon. For a small company with a limited supply of actors, keeping the Induction, then fading it out at the end of I.i. and recycling the actors in other parts may well be the most economically feasible decision.

The majority of professional directors, however (most of whom have not had to worry about a limited supply of actors), have chosen to keep the Presenters on stage throughout the play so as to never let the audience forget that they are watching a play-within-a-play, and to emphasize that "distancing" and "softening" effect described earlier in this essay. Quite a few directors have taken their cue from Quiller-Couch, who theorized that Shakespeare deliberately omitted any further lines for Sly, intending that the actor who played him feel free to extemporize and comment (verbally or non-verbally) on the action taking place before him.[29]

Left to his own devices to comment on and participate in the play, the actor playing Sly (with, of course, the coaching of the director) has many choices. He can react non-verbally throughout the play, as D. Hay Petrie did so successfully in Andrew Leigh's 1917 production at the Lyric Theatre, prompting *The London Times* reviewer to exclaim: "His is an extraordinarily good piece of acting, notable for the industry with which, condemned to silence, he presses the members of his body into the service of eloquence. His lips, his eyebrows, his fingers are admirably expressive; his lusty motions of applause and his silent confidences are a weightier commentary than words."[30] Or he can verbalize his reactions, as M. Donnio did in Gremier's

1924 French production in New York City, bursting out irreverently in English slang whenever he felt so moved. He can wander around the stage to get a better view, as in George Devine's 1953 and 1954 Stratford-upon-Avon productions, and occasionally participate directly in the slapstick: he can assist in whacking Grumio (Guthrie's 1939 Old Vic production), steal a whiskey bottle from one of the players with a butterfly net, Harpo Marx fashion (Norman Lloyd's 1955 Stratford, Connecticut production), or he can rush on stage — much to the consternation of the Lord — to join the wedding feast at Baptista's house (Michael Langham's 1962 Stratford, Ontario production). The possibilities for Sly's active participation are many, and interestingly enough, his antics always appear to add to rather than detract from the audience's focus on the play proper; I found not one review where an extemporizing Sly was accused of upstaging the Shrew story. On the contrary, many reviewers considered Sly the hit of the show and devoted more space to praising him than any of the other principals. Sly's particular appeal, most reviewers agree, is his childlike sense of wonder and enchantment, which adds immeasurably to the audience's own enjoyment of the play. A typical example is *The London Times* reviewer's assessment of Bernard Miles's performance as Sly in John Burrell's 1947 production at the New Theatre: "The whole action is warmed through with the good-natured fellow's childlike, if flamingly bibulous, appreciation of its simple excitements and all the brutality is warmed out of it. With the tinker and his mock wife aloft on a great bed, surrounded by the sportive nobleman and his amused friends, the play enacted on the floor below them becomes an Elizabethan romp. The tinker's delight in his entertainment, never relaxed and never overdone by Mr. Bernard Miles, communicates itself irresistibly. . . ."[31]

So theatrically appealing has Sly's presence been to some directors that they have chosen to pad out his part by including sections from *The Taming of a Shrew*. Harcourt Williams appears to have been the first (in 1931) to add the Epilogue from *A Shrew*, and since that time, although most scholars have defended Shakespeare's choice (if, indeed, it was his choice) to omit an epilogue (they condsider it too anti-climactic[32]), the directors who have chosen to follow Williams' example — notably Tyrone Guthrie (1939), John Burrell (1947), Margaret Webster (1951), George Devine (1954), Craig Noel (1962), Michael Langham (1962), and Trevor Nunn (1967) — have met with marked success. *The London Times* reviewer of Ben Iden-Payne's 1936 production at Stratford-upon-Avon, for example, felt that "the dovetailing of the two pieces is . . . harmless and even necessary. It sets the comedy more firmly in what seems to be its proper place, and it sends us away with echoes of something better than Kate's clap-trap about the duties which a wife owes to her husband, lord, and master."[33] George Devine was also praised for his "judicious use" of the epilogue from *A Shrew*, which enabled him "to cover the central crudity in as many separate wrappings of illusion as it will bear."[34] The Epilogue not only contributes to the "rounding off" of the play, but also, as Arnold Edinborough, reviewing Langham's 1962 production, noted, to the highlighting of the central irony of the play, that "only on the stage do men wive it wealthily and/or happily."[35]

It must be stressed that the decision to keep Sly on stage throughout the play does not necessarily force the director into a no-holds-barred, anything goes, boisterously farcical production. Although W. Bridges-Adams refused to have anything to do with Sly during his tenure as director of the Stratford-upon-Avon Shakespeare Festival from 1920 to 1933, asserting that Kate and Petruchio would certainly dislike "having twenty preoccupied and irrelevant types round them on the stage — to say nothing of a bed — at that perfectly thrumming moment when they are alone together for the first time,"[36] most directors who choose to keep Sly find, as Richard David noted about George Devine's 1954 production, that "at any moment (such is the flexibility of drama) the play can soar out of its framework, which drops away and is forgotten in the instant."[37] In spite of (or with the assistance of) Sly on the stage, Kate and Petruchio can fall in love at first sight, or on the way home from their "honeymoon," or at the end of the play, or never. Kate can give her last speech ironically (with a knowing wink to the audience or to Sly), or conspiratorily (with a knowing wink to Petruchio), or absolutely sincerely (and then Sly winks at *us* — after all, it's *his* dream). The play proper can be performed as all-out farce or romantic comedy or a happy combination of both. And any production can be panned for going too far in any direction, with or without the assistance of Sly.

What matters most, then, is the additional level of illusion which Sly's presence adds to our appreciation of the play on the stage. In the study, we may quickly forget all about Sly after I.i., but in the theatre, if the director has retained him, we will be made constantly aware of what J. Denis Huston has called Shakespeare's "hall of mirrors" effect:

> *Shakespeare begins a play, which is then apparently re-begun as a more conventional play, in which a Lord decides to stage a play, but he is interrupted by a group of players, who themselves come to offer service in the form of a play to this Lord, who talks with them about yet another play, which they have acted in the past but which they are not going to present this evening, when a player-Lord will observe their performance of a play staged after the 'real' Lord and his servants have played out their play with the player-Lord, who will [possibly] sleep through the play which Shakespeare, himself playing through this mind-boggling series of false starts, will utimately present to his audience.*[38]

The play can be — has frequently been — a hit without Christopher Sly. But something is always lost.

## TABLE I

### Productions of *The Taming of the Shrew*

| Director/Producer | Date | Place | Cut Induction | Keep Induction | Sly disappears after I.ii (or just falls asleep) | Sly stays on stage (and reacts) | Sly doubled |
|---|---|---|---|---|---|---|---|
| Benjamin Webster | 1844 | Haymarket | | X | | X | |
| Samuel Phelps | 1856 | Sadler's Well | | X | X | | |
| Augustin Daly | 1887; revived 1889, 1891, 1894, 1897 1904, 1905 | Daly's NYC (and on tour) | | X | X | | |
| F.R. Benson | 1890-1916 | Globe, Shakes. Mem. Th., Stratford | X | | | | |
| Oscar Asche | 1904 | Adelphi | | X | X | | X w/Pet |
| E. H. Sothern & Julia Marlowe | 1905 | Knickerbocker Th., NC | X | | | | |
| Novelli (Italian Co.) | 1907 | Lyric, NYC | X | | | | |
| Max Reinhardt | 1909 | Deutsches Th., Berlin | | X | | X | |
| Martin Harvey | 1913 | Prince of Wales Th. | | X | | X | |
| Margaret Anglin | 1914 | Hudson Th., NYC | X | | | | |
| Rudolph Christians (German Co.) | 1916 | Irving Place. Th., NYC | | X | | X | |
| Walter Hampden | 1921 | Broadhurst Th., NYC | X | | | | |
| M. Gremier (French Co.) | 1924 | Johnson's 59th St. Th., NYC | | X | | X | |
| Richard Boleslavsky | 1925 | Klaw Th., NYC | X | | | | |
| Edith Evans & Balliol Holloway | 1925 | Old Vic | | X | X | | |
| Andrew Leigh | 1927 | Lyric Th., England | | X | | X | |

**TABLE I (continued)**

| Director/Producer | Date | Place | Cut Induction | Keep Induction | Sly disappears after I.ii (or just falls asleep) | Sly stays on stage (and reacts) | Sly doubled |
|---|---|---|---|---|---|---|---|
| H. K. Ayliff (Garrick Players) | 1927 | Garrick Th., NYC | | X | | X | |
| Barry Jackson | 1928 | Court Th., London | | X | | X | |
| Fritz Leiber | 1930 | Schubert Th., NYC | | X | X | | X w/Pet |
| Harcourt Williams | 1931 | Sadler's Wells | | X | | X | |
| Henry Cass | 1934 | Sadler's Wells | | X | X | | |
| Lunt & Fontanne | 1935 | Theatre Guild, NYC | | X | | X | |
| Ben Iden Payne | 1936 | Stratford | | X | | X | |
| Claud Gurney | 1937 | New Theatre, London | | X | X | | X w/Pedant |
| Tyrone Guthrie | 1939 | Old Vic | | X | | X | |
| Theodore Komisarjevsky | 1939 | Stratford | | X | | X | |
| Ben Iden Payne | 1940 | Stratford | | X | | X | |
| John Burrell | 1947 | Lyceum | | X | | X | |
| Michael Benthall | 1948 | Stratford | | X | | X | |
| Margaret Webster | 1951 | NY City Center | | X | | X | X w/horse |
| George Devine | 1953 | Stratford | | X | | X | X w/horse |
| George Devine | 1954 | Stratford | | X | | X | X w/horse |
| Tyrone Guthrie | 1954 | Stratford, Ontario | | X | | X | |
| Denis Carey | 1954 | Old Vic | | X | | X | |
| Norman Lloyd | 1955 | Stratford, Conn. | | X | | X | |
| Norman Lloyd | 1956 | Stratford | | X | | X | |
| John Barton | 1960 | Stratford | | X | | X | |
| Joseph Papp | 1960 | Central Park, NYC | | X | | X | |
| Maurice Daniels | 1961 | Aldwych, London | | X | | X | |
| Craig Noel | 1962 | Old Globe Th., San Diego | | X | | X | |
| Michael Langham | 1962 | Stratford, Ontario | | X | | X | |

**TABLE I (continued)**

| Director/Producer | Date | Place | Cut Induction | Keep Induction | Sly disappears after I.ii (or just falls asleep) | Sly stays on stage (and reacts) | Sly doubled |
|---|---|---|---|---|---|---|---|
| Stuart Vaughan | 1963 | NYC, Phyllis Anderson Th. | X | | | | |
| Joseph Anthony | 1965 | Straftord, Conn. | X | | | | |
| Trevor Nunn | 1967 | RSC | | X | | X | |
| Robert Benedetti | 1969 | Colorado Shakes. Festival | X | | | | |
| Michael Langham | 1971 | Guthrie Th. | | X | | X | |
| Jonathan Miller | 1972 | Chicester | X | | | | |
| Paul Barry | 1972 | New Jersey Shakes. Festival | | X | X | | |
| Clifford Williams | 1973 | RSC, Stratford | | X | X | | |
| Clifford Williams | 1973 | Stratford, Ontario | X | | | | |
| Dunlop (Young Vic Co.) | 1974 | On Tour in NYC | | X | | X | X w/Pedant |
| Frank Dwyer | 1974 | Monmouth, Maine | | X | | X | |
| Barnet Kellman | 1977 | North Carolina Shakes. Festival | X | | | | |
| Daniel Sullivan | 1978 | Great Lakes Shakes. Festival | | X | | X | |
| Brian Hansen | 1978 | Utah Shakes. Festival | | X | | X | |
| Laird Williamson | $978 | San Diego Shakes. Festival | | X | | X | |
| Wilford Leach | 1978 | New York Shakes. Festival | | X | | X | |
| Michael Bogdanov | 1978 | Stratford | | X | X | | X Sly & Pet. |
| John Davis | 1978 | Virginia Shakes. Festival | | X | | | |
| R. O. Ceballos | 1978 | Shakes. Festival of Cinn. | X | | | | |
| Judd Parkin | 1978 | Oregon Shakes. Festival | X | | | | |
| Gerhard Klingenberg | 1978 | Zurich, Switz. | | X | | X | |

## NOTES

[1]Induction, ii. 17-19. From *The Taming of the Shrew*, edited by G. L. Kittredge, rev. ed. by Irving Ribner (Waltham, Massachusetts: Blaisdell Publishing Company, 1966). All references are to this edition.

[2]For a sample of the thematic approaches to the Induction see: Thelma Greenfied, "The Transformation of Christopher Sly," *Philological Quarterly* 33 (1954), 34-42; William J. Martz, *Shakespeare's Universe of Comedy* (N.Y.: David Lewis, 1971), p. 57; J. Denis Huston, " 'To Make a Puppet': Play and Playmaking in *The Taming of the Shrew*," *Shakespeare Studies* 9 (1976), 73-87.

[3]*The Diary of Samuel Pepys*, edited by Richard Lord Braybrooke (London: Frederick Warne and Company, 1800), p. 378.

[4]See Harold Child, "The Stage History of *The Taming of the Shrew*," in the New Cambridge Edition, edited by Arthur Quiller-Couch and J. Dover Wilson (Cambridge: Cambridge University Press, 1928; rpt. 1968), pp. 181-86.

[5]*The New York Times*, Oct. 22, 1905, pt. 3, p. 2.

[6]*The New York Times*, Dec. 19, 1925, p. 14.

[7]*Shakespeare Quarterly* 30 (1979), p. 210.

[8]See *Eyewitnesses of Shakespeare*, ed. Gamini Salgado (N.Y.: Harper and Row, 1975), p. 75.

[9]*The Athenaeum*, Mar. 18, 1844, p. 5.

[10]*The London Times*, Mar. 18, 1844, p. 5.

[11]Larry S. Champion, *The Evolution of Shakespeare's Comedies* (Cambridge, Mass.: Harvard University Press, 1970), p. 39.

[12]Robert Speaight, *Shakespeare on the Stage* (Boston: Little, Brown & Co., 1973), p. 204.

[13]Tyrone Guthrie, Robertson Davies and Grant Macdonald, *Twice Have the Trumpets Sounded: A Record of the Stratford Shakespearean Festival in Canada, 1954* (Toronto: Clarke, Irwin and Co., 1954), p. 58.

[14]*The London Times*, May 12, 1913, p. 8.

[15]*The London Times*, Oct. 14, 1921, p. 10.

[16]*Shakespeare Quarterly* 5 (1954), p. 393.

[17]*The London Times*, July 8, 1940, p. 6.

[18]*The London Times*, Aug. 27, 1947, p. 6.

[19]*Punch*, Apr. 12, 1967, p. 539.

[20]*Shakespeare Quarterly* 13 (1962), p. 522.

[21]*The Examiner*, Dec. 6, 1856. Quoted in *The Life and Life-Work of Samuel Phelps*, by W. May Phelps and John Forbes-Robertson (London: Sampson, Low, Marston, Searle and Ribington, 1886), p. 155.

[22]*The Athenaeum*, June 2, 1888, p. 706.

[23]*The London Times*, Jan. 2, 1935, p. 8.

[24]Introduction to the New Cambridge Edition, p. xviii.

[25]Notes to the New Cambridge Edition, p. 142.

[26]Introduction to the Folio Society Edition (1960), p. 7.

[27]*The New York Times*, July 16, 1978, p. 4. For other reviews of this production, see *Shakespeare Survey* 32 (1979), 201-202; *Theatre Journal* 32 (1980), 122-23; *Plays and Players* 25 (1978), 29; *Shakespeare Quarterly* 30 (1979), 152-54.

[28]Sears Jayne has devised an imaginative solution to the problem of doubling Sly and Petruchio. See "The Dreaming of the *Shrew*," *Shakespeare Quarterly* 17 (1966), 41-56.

[29]Introduction to the New Cambridge Edition, p. xxv.

[30]*The London Times*, Dec. 20, 1927, P. 12.

[31]*The London TImes*, Nov. 5, 1947, p. 7.

[32]See Richard Hosley, "Was There a 'Dramatic Epilogue' to *The Taming of the Shrew*?" *Studies in English Literature* 1.2 (1961), 17-34; and Ernest P. Kuhl, "Shakespeare's Purpose in Dropping Sly," *Modern Language Notes* 36 (1921), 321-27. For the opposite viewpoint, see Peter Alexander. "The Original Ending of *Shrew*," *Shakespeare Quarterly* 20 (1969), 111-116.

[33]*The London Times*, April 14, 1936, p. 8.

[34]*The London Times*, June 2, 1954, p. 2.
[35]*Shakespeare Survey* 16 (1963), p. 152.
[36]From a letter to Arthur Colby Sprague, printed in *A Bridges-Adams Letter Book*, ed. Robert Speaight (N.Y.: Society for Theatre Research, 1970-71), p. 63.
[37]*Shakespeare Quarterly* 5 (1954), p. 394.
[38]Huston, p. 81.

# George Jean Nathan and the "New Criticism"

TICE L. MILLER

"Biased criticism is not the less despicable because it praises."
*Smart Set*, November 1910

In the decade prior to World War One, a growing number of critics — literary, dramatic, music, art — took the measure of American culture and found it sadly out of touch with contemporary life and lagging behind what was happening in Europe. Attitudes which had permeated American society from the Civil War continued to shape the nation's literature and art. Best selling novelists Harold Bell Wright, Rex Beach, and Gene Stratton-Porter, ignored the harsh realities of industrial America and provided their readers with sentimental romances. Contrived melodramas by Augustus Thomas, Clyde Fitch, Charles Klein, and David Belasco filled the theatres. The reigning "Genteel" critics had fled to the sanctuary of the Century Club where they issued proclamations about an idealized and perfumed art which did not concern itself with the vulgar or trivial. But the old order was passing, pushed aside by a new generation who demanded a closer relationship between art and experience. During the 1910s and 1920s, one of the most important and influential of the new school was dramatic critic George Jean Nathan. Writing mainly in the *Smart Set* and later the *American Mercury*, Nathan attacked Puritanism in American art and letters, and commercialism in the theatre. His criticism set the tone for native theatre journalism in the second and third decades of the twentieth century.

Born at Fort Wayne, Indiana, on February 14, 1882, George Jean Nathan grew up in an environment where education, travel, literature, and art were prized.[1] His parents were wealthy. At an early age, he was provided with a private tutor, and later was sent to Cornell University where he graduated in 1904. After travel and further schooling in Europe, he began a two-year stint as reporter and third-string reviewer for the *New York Herald*, a job secured through the efforts of an uncle, Charles Frederic Nirdlinger. He then obtained his first post as dramatic critic for two little magazines, *Outing* and *The Bohemian*, and began contributing theatrical essays to major magazines: *Harper's Weekly, Munsey's,* and *Burr McIntosh*. The young journalist exhibited a fine talent for writing, including a unique style. By the time he began as dramatic critic for *Smart Set* in October, 1909, he had served a profitable apprenticeship.

A chic monthly magazine, *Smart Set* had been founded in 1900 by publisher Colonel William D'Alton Mann to offer fictionized accounts of the upper classes in a light, frivolous manner.[2] Its purpose was to entertain,

Tice L. Miller is Professor of Theatre Arts at the University of Nebraska-Lincoln.

however, not to reform. Through most of its first decade, it competed for circulation with the snobbish *Ainslee's* magazine. Internal scandal and financial losses, however, prompted its editors to push for new directions in 1908. They persuaded H. L. Mencken from Baltimore to write a book review column. A year later when Channing Pollock resigned from the dramatic post, they hired George Jean Nathan to replace him. It was clear that Mencken and Nathan provided the *Smart Set* with some of the liveliest writing in New York. The new dramatic critic wrote his first review for the October, 1909, issue and remained at the post for the next fifteen years. For ten of those years, he and Mencken also served as the *Smart Set's* co-editors.

There was much to criticize in the American theatre of 1909. The Genteel Tradition had required propriety and moral purity rather than vitality and honesty in the drama. In 1909 the Shuberts and the Theatrical Syndicate were fighting for control of the American stage. Instead of concerning themselves with theatre which explored metaphysical and social problems, they manufactured entertainment for the nation through assembly line methods. While they did not oppose art, it had to show a profit. In their efforts to increase business, they spent large sums of money on advertising. As a result, newspaper critics faced intense pressure to speak favorably about their productions. Between 1905-1915, three prominent New York critics — Acton Davies of the *Sun*, Alan Dale of the *American*, and William Winter of the *Tribune* — were fired from their jobs. Numerous essays were printed about the loss of critical independence. Writing for *Smart Set*, Nathan did not face such pressures. There is no evidence that he pulled his punches for fear of being fired.

At the beginning of his career, George Jean Nathan offered little more than gossip and theatrical chit-chat in his theatrical column. His first article for *Smart Set* (October 1909) was a worthless piece, "Why We Fall in Love with Actresses." The following month his second, "The Drama Comes into Season," was self-consciously cute and clever — much like Alan Dale's writing for Hearst publications. Nathan's judgment at this time was suspect. Like most of his contemporaries, he was overly-enthusiastic about Clyde Fitch's *The City*: "All other recent sensationally built plays are lost far beneath in its shadows" (February 1910). Belasco's *The Lily* he called "another mark of honor on the Belasco coat-of-arms. . . . " (March 1910). He found worth in Pinero's *Mid-Channel* (1910) and Charles Klein's *The Gamblers* (1911), although admitting the following year that he had overestimated the quality of Klein's play, Nathan would later confess to youthful indiscretion and poor judgment in his early career. But he reserved the right to change his mind; critics who held to the same opinions throughout their careers he termed bad critics. It was not until the 1912-1913 season that his taste gave evidence of maturity.

The critic James Huneker proved a strong influence on Nathan's early career.[3] An outspoken foe of the "Genteel Tradition" and of American literature in particular, Huneker interested the younger critic in the philosophy of Friedrich Nietzsche, and in the new European drama of Ibsen, Shaw, and Hauptmann. He shunned academic criticism in favor of a lively, impressionistic style where the bon mot reigned supreme. Nathan followed his lead, as did colleague H. L. Mencken, who also wrote in a witty and satirical style with ridicule a major weapon against literary foolishness. Legend grew up around the pair, fueled in part by the writers themselves. Their co-editorship of *Smart Set* (1914-1924) and for a time in 1924 of *The American Mercury* must be regarded as an important milestone in the development of American arts and letters. They were first-rate editors. Carl Dolmetsch in a recent article gives credit to both for "spotting literary talent and for sniffing out the kind of cleverness and insouciance the two editors admired."[4] They offered publishing opportunities for a new generation of writers — Willa Cather and F. Scott Fitzgerald for two — and encouraged young playwrights, designers, directors, and critics.

Compared to the elder statesmen of the trade — William Winter and J. Ranken Towse — Nathan wrote more readable and entertaining prose. His extensive vocabulary included French as well as newly coined words from either his or Mencken's pen: "Piffle", "flapdoodle", "pish-posh" and "bozart." The *Smart Set's* dramatic column provided its readers with a level of sophistication not matched by its rivals. While Nathan's older colleagues, Davies and Dale, had attained popularity through a colorful style designed to attract the masses, neither could match his verve. His epigrams frequently resembled a concoction of Oscar Wilde and Bernard Shaw: "We Americans are a patriotic people — we are loyal Englishmen."

After finding his critical voice in *Smart Set*, Nathan launched a blistering attack upon what he regarded as dry rot in the American theatre. He ignored advice to be a sympathetic and constructive critic. The problem with native reviewers, he noted, is their incapacity to dispraise. Despite the vast amount of laudatory comments bestowed upon each season's offerings, he seldom found more than five or six shows which merited critical attention. The rest he regarded as "trick melodramas, fussy farces, mob much, leg shows." The level of taste among American audiences, he thought to be at a deplorable level. On one hand "Uplifters" wanted to improve public taste with morally pure shows; on the other hand regular theatregoers demanded their own thoughts and emotions reflected on the stage. Neither group wished for new ideas. The commercial theatre catered to these groups by offering a repetition of stock morality, stock characters, stock plot situations and manufactured "stars." Stale theatrical fare came to be expected, even enjoyed, by audiences as Nathan noted on one occasion in 1918: "Any scene however badly written, in which an actor comes out on the stage carrying a dog that is supposed to have been run over by a motor car driven by the villain, will set the audience to polyphonous sniffling and to an almost audible vituperation of the heinous chauffeur."[5] Producers offered such pap, he concluded, because that is what mob taste demands.

Debunking the sacred idols of the 1910s occupied most of his *Smart Set* criticism. David Belasco, considered by many (including William Winter) to be an outstanding innovator, came to symbolize much of what Nathan thought was wrong with the American stage: "It is the general producing technique of David Belasco first to pick out as poor a play as he can find and then assiduously to devote his talents to distracting the audience's attention from its mediocrity."[6] He accused Belasco of impressing the audience with realistic detail and not concerning himself with the whole production. Nathan stated the situation another way in his review of *Little Lady in Blue*: "To applaud the practice of Mr. David Belasco in expending infinite care and time in perfecting the production of so empty and bootless a play as *Little Lady in Blue,* is akin to an admiration for the sort of adult who triumphantly expends painstaking effort and time in putting together the several hundred little pieces of a jigsaw puzzle."[7] On another occasion, Nathan called Belasco "a polisher of peanuts: a producer who produces with brilliant effect things not worth producing." Nathan thought it ridiculous to compare him to Antoine or Stanislavsky or Reinhardt whom he regarded as true theatrical innovators.

His review of *The Return of Peter Grimm* (*Smart Set,* December 1911) reveals critical methods which were to prove effective in demolishing the Belasco drama. "One minute after the fall of the final curtain . . . the average cool-minded and normally perceptive spectator is quite positive that he has just witnessed the exploitation of a profound contribution to native drama. One hour after the fall of the final curtain his suspicions begin to become aroused. And one day after the fall of the final curtain he is quite positive that what he witnessed was exactly one part profound drama to ninety-nine parts profound theatrical trickery." While complimenting Belasco on his ability to keep "common sense at bay for one whole, long day," the critic expressed dismay with the "flimsy fabric of the play." The piece dealt with the return of the title character from the grave. Belasco had attempted to explain away its lack of logic through a program note: "For the many, it may be said that he [Peter Grimm] could exist only in the minds of the characters grouped about him — in their subconscious memories. For the few, his presence will embody the theory of the survival of persistent personal energy. The character has, so far as possible, been treated to accord with either thought." In light of the play, Nathan found such statements ridiculous: "Peter Grimm, upon his return into the play after death, indulges himself (or his spirit) in hitherto unspoken and unacted thoughts, in principles contradictory to those he held while life was yet in him. How then could he exist in the subconscious memories of the characters and dominate the characters with constant changes of thought and thereby impel them to deeds of contrariety?" And as to the "survival of persistent personal energy theory," Nathan pointed out that Belasco's handling of the plot conflicted with the best scientific information on this matter. He concluded that *The Return of Peter Grimm* was but a triumph of Belasco stage art, not a triumph of dramatic and scientific logic. Reduced to "terms of Broadway," the play was merely an "amplified dramatization of the Ghost in *Hamlet*." Such systematic dismantling of plays and productions came to be a Nathan trademark.

Belasco then had contributed but one thing worthy of judicious praise: "He had brought to that [American] theatre a standard of tidiness in production and maturation of manuscript, a standard that has discouraged to no little extent that theatre's erstwhile not uncommon frowzy hustle and slipshod manner of presentation."[8] But against this one accomplishment, Nathan continued, he must be judged for failing to produce any classics; for ignoring first-rate English, French, and German plays; for failing to encourage any young American talent; for creating a system where playwrights are rewarded for writing only sure-fire hits. Nathan concluded that he had done nothing to assist the drama as a fine art. By comparison, commercial producers Charles Frohman and Winthrop Ames had made more worthwhile contributions to the American stage.

Nathan regarded the American drama before Eugene O'Neill as a vast desert created by a system which understood only commercial ends. Not only Belasco, but also Bronson Howard, James A. Herne, Clyde Fitch, Charles Klein, Augustus Thomas, George Broadhurst, and Charles Rann Kennedy were no better than third and fourth-rate playwrights. The demands of the commercial stage encouraged them to build successful plays rather than to reflect life in a vital way. Nathan came to abhore their slavish adherence to the well-made formula. Rules for playwriting he thought unimportant: "A writer should center his mind upon something besides entrances and exits." He especially hated the obligatory "Big Scene" which appeared in every play. Albert Thomas wrote an obligatory sentimental scene for his *The Rainbow* (1919), which Nathan thought was carefully manufactured to "twang tears from your heart strings . . . although why you will cry I am sure I cannot say." George Broadhurst's *Bought and Paid For,* a huge financial success, Nathan dismissed as inconsequential and sensational: "Mr. Broadhurst causes the husband to smash in the door of the room after the wife has locked herself in. This smashing in of a door is invariably regarded as 'great stuff' in our drama. It can always be relied upon to produce a deep affect on an audience."[9] William Gillette had built a fortune on the same effect; and it was used whenever a playwright found himself in trouble: "The smashed door is to the theater of Broadway what the snowstorm and a view of the Brooklyn Bridge by moonlight is the the theater of Third Avenue."[10]

Charles Rann Kennedy, also, was not immune from such practices. In reviewing *The Terrible Meek* (1912), Nathan accused the playwright of substituting theatrical trickery for thought: "He causes a fifty-minute long play to be enacted on a completely darkened stage before an audience in a completely darkened auditorium, and then, when the play is ended, he sits back figuratively and smiles a broad smile of satisfaction for having succeeded in 'impressing' that audience. But he never appears to stop to think that it was not his play that impressed his audience nearly so much as the fact that he had compelled the persons in it to sit for nearly an hour in weird and shivery surroundings."[11] Such claptrap would continue to plague the American drama until audiences demanded something besides sensational melodrama. "The American people love, honor, and obey melodrama above every other form of dramatic art," Nathan believed.[12] A nation's cultural sophistication, he concluded, depends upon the respect it *does not* hold for melodrama.

The American public also demanded a steady fare of "theatrical romances of love." Nathan explained, however, that there were only four acceptable ways of packaging the topic for native tastes: one, a poor but virtuous "Maggie Pepper or Virginia Blaine" is pursued by a rich cavalier; two, an already married "delicious morsel" wins back a husband "devoting too much time to business and too little to stroking her hair"; three, a girl who has "gone wrong" is forgiven and loved by a good man; and, four, a "self-sufficient female" and her two wooers joust until the illogical gentleman wins her hand at eleven o'clock because "he happens to be the leading man."[13] Nathan concluded that the women in the audience dictated these shopworn love plots, and warned playwrights: "No matter how sublime an ass a woman may be, no matter what she thinks or feels or does not feel, hug her at the end — or your play will fail."[14]

With a reputation for harshly censoring much of the drama of his day, it is important to note that Nathan encouraged playwrights whom he thought had the capacity and courage for honest work. He regarded Bernard Shaw as a genius — a man capable of filling any play with important ideas. Shaw's *Man and Superman, Candida,* and *Arms and the Man,* he listed among his favorite plays. Yet he did not find the Englishman to be a revolutionary thinker: "Much of what was accepted as daring had already long been tried and tested when Shaw offered it."[15] Shaw's talent lay in his ability to "restate platitudes in such a manner that their weariness left them and that they took on again the color of youth." While he laughed at the old conventions of the drama, nevertheless he kept them and "by playing his wit over them, gaily deceived his willing customers that they were right out of the bandbox."[16]

Nathan became Eugene O'Neill's early and most ardent champion in the press. His interest in the playwright went beyond critical support: he introduced O'Neill to New Yorkers in 1918 by publishing three of his one-act pieces in *Smart Set;* he was responsible for arranging a professional production of the playwright's first full-length work, *Beyond the Horizon,* in 1920. The two men became close friends. Nathan used his position as a major critic to encourage interest in O'Neill's work. In 1920 he predicted a brilliant future for the writer, noting his desire to pursue important themes and his strong sense of character.[17] After O'Neill's death, Nathan wrote at length about *Long Day's Journey into Night,* calling it tragic writing which raised life into a plane "that gives it a size beyond itself."[18] Their extant correspondence at Cornell and Yale suggests that Nathan offered practical advice about money and playwriting; criticism when he found evidence of shoddy work; but mainly encouragement for O'Neill to write plays with size and dimension. Nathan wanted an American drama which could compete in the world market with the best of Europe. George Freedley later wrote that Nathan together with Mencken, "did more to improve the standard of serious dramatic writing in this country than any single writer who was not primarily a playwright himself."[19]

The Victorians, William Winter and J. Ranken Towse, had considered acting the highest theatrical art. Nathan took an opposite view: "I believe . . . that altogether too much attention is paid the actor on all occasions, and that, on all occasions, it ought to be remembered that the artistic dramatic relation of the actor to the play is in the ratio of one to one thousand."[20] He did not regard acting as a worthy art because the actor must be popular or perish: "The actor, save on rare occasions, is not logically an artist and cannot conduct himself as one." His attitude on this issue differed little from popular newspaper critics Stephen Fiske, Alan Dale, and Acton Davies who described acting as a derivative art.

It was not that Nathan hated actors nor failed to appreciate fine acting, but he expected the actor to put the play and role before anything else. This he seldom found. He reacted adversely to press agent puffery, and found offensive, actors commenting glibly in the press about world and domestic affairs: "Let them occupy such misspent time in thinking about that foreign and seemingly irrelevant thing called acting," he demanded. And he expected a critic to evaluate the actor on his performance, not on his looks, personality, personal life, or clothes. Nathan believed that Eleonora Duse was a superstar of the theatre because she worked hard at her craft, always placed herself subservient to the role, and made her body the tool of her mind.[21] He criticized Mrs. Fiske for drawing attention to herself through statements to the press, rather than concentrating on her acting. He thought John Barrymore's Hamlet was weakened by "self-consciousness" of the occasion and of tradition.[22] The actor's job is to portray the character. "Let our actors go nameless," Nathan concluded. "Let our actors cease to be incandescent lights and pictured endorsers of O'Sullivan's Rubber Heels . . . and let them become roles, characters etched into plays, figures in moving narratives, elements for the assisting of drama on its respectable course."[23] His views on the subject were, at times, as dogmatic as Gordon Craig's who wanted to replace the actor with the marionette to get silence and obedience.

Nathan demanded that all elements of a production serve the drama. He condemned directors who exploited plays to demonstrate their own techniques and style: "Among directors both big and little the world over, one finds this vain adherence to and exposition of an inflexible technique or style. . . ."[24] Thus one does not need to look at the playbill to know a Stanislavsky production, or a Jessner, or a Copeau, or a Belasco, or even an Arthur Hopkins; their directing personality is always present. Among modern directors Nathan believed only Max Reinhardt devised a new technique for each separate drama: "There is not one director Reinhardt — there are a dozen director Reinhardts." The director is merely a tool to fashion the playwright's monument, not vice versa.

And critics should abandon all theories, Nathan advocated: "There are as many sound and apt species of criticism as there are works to be criticized."[25] He believed that each work of art is an entity and must be criticized as a thing in itself. Goethe's theory that a critic should discover what is being done, how it is being done, and whether it was worth doing, Nathan regarded as only a foundation for a critical philosophy. "Criticism, as I see it," he wrote in 1922, "is simply a sensitive, experienced, and thoroughbred artist's effort to interpret, in terms of aesthetic doctrine and his own peculiar soul, the work of another artist reciprocally to that artist and thus, as with a reflecting mirror, to his public."[26] He thought it unimportant whether criticism conformed to one system of aesthetics or another; what *was* important is that the critic have taste and experience.

Nathan's criticism in the 1910s and early 1920s remains his most worthwhile contribution to the American stage. He introduced to American audiences the best of modern European dramatists; he encouraged young native playwrights; and he helped change the public's attitude toward the theatre and drama. While he gained power and prestige in his mature years as "Dean of American Drama Critics" his early career left a more indelible mark on the American theatre. The George Jean Nathan Award for Dramatic Criticism given annually from a trust set up by his will, continues as an ongoing effort to encourage "the art of drama criticism" and to stimulate "Intelligent Playgoing."[27]

## NOTES

[1]For information about Nathan's life and career see: Constance Frick, *The Dramatic Criticism of George Jean Nathan* (Ithaca, New York: Cornell University Press, 1943); Thomas Quinn Curtiss, ed., *The Magic Mirror: Selected Writings on the Theatre by George Jean Nathan* (New York: Alfred A. Knopf, 1960); Isaac Goldberg, *The Theatre of George Jean Nathan* (New York: Simon and Schuster, 1926); Charles Angoff, ed., *The World of George Jean Nathan* (New York: Alfred A. Knopf, 1952); Herbert M. Simpson, "Mencken and Nathan," Diss., University of Maryland, 1965; Seymour Rudin, "George Jean Nathan: A Study of His Criticism," Diss., Cornell University, 1953; Arthur Salvatore Ruffino, "A Cumulative Index to the Books of George Jean Nathan," Diss., Southern Illinois University, 1971. Nathan's papers may be examined at The Rare Book Room, Cornell University Library; Patricia Angelin, New York City, is the Literary Executrix of the Nathan Estate.

[2]For a history of the *Smart Set* see: Carl R. Dolmetsch, *The Smart Set: a History and Anthology* (New York: The Dial Press, 1966).

[3]See Arnold T. Schwab, *James Gibbon Huneker: Critic of the Seven Arts* (Palo Alto: Stanford University Press, 1963).

[4]Carl Dolmetsch, " 'HLM and GJN:' The Editorial Partnership Re-examined," *Menckeniana*, Fall 1980, p. 32.

[5]George Jean Nathan, *The Popular Theatre* (New York: Alfred A. Knopf, 1918), p. 23.

[6]George Jean Nathan, *Comedians All* (New York: Alfred A. Knopf, 1919), p. 217.

[7]George Jean Nathan, *Mr. George Jean Nathan Presents* (New York: Alfred A. Knopf, 1917), p. 66.

[8]*Ibid.*, p. 76.

[9]*Smart Set*, December 1911, p. 146.

[10]*Ibid.*

[11]*Smart Set*, June 1912, P. 150.

[12]*Smart Set*, November 1913, p. 145.

[13]*Smart Set*, January 1912, p. 146.

[14]*Ibid.*

[15]Quoted in *The Magic Mirror*, p. 174.

[16]*Ibid.*

[17]*Smart Set*, July 1920, p. 132.

[18]New York *Journal-American*, November 8, 1956. O'Neill clipping folder, Billy Rose Theatre Collection of The New York Public Library at Lincoln Center.

[19]*New York Morning Telegraph*, April 26, 1958.

[20]*Smart Set*, August 1913, p. 148.

[21]George Jean Nathan, *Materia Criteria* (1924; rpt. Rutherford: Fairleigh Dickinson University Press, 1971), p. 167.

22 *Ibid.*, p. 180.
23 *Smart Set*, March 1913, p. 146.
24 Quoted in *The Magic Mirror*, pp. 74-78.
25 Quoted in *The Magic Mirror*, p. 33.
26 *Ibid.*, p. 36.
27 Printed brochure describing the award by The Manufacturers Hanover Trust, New York City, administrators of the Nathan Estate. Misc. folder, Nathan Collection, Cornell University Library.

# Notes and Queries

# T. W. Robertson's Early Contempt for the Theatre: A Newly Discovered Letter

DANIEL BARRETT

Tucked into the manuscript of his "lost" play, *Down in Our Village*, at the Stanford University Libraries is a revealing letter by the playwright T. W. Robertson (1829-71) written shortly before his emergence as London's leading dramatist in the late 1860s.[1] Robertson had moved to London in 1849 after the Lincoln Circuit company run by his parents succumbed to financial pressures and disbanded. For the next eleven years he worked periodically as a light comedian, prompter, and stage manager for metropolitan, provincial, and touring companies. He also wrote plays — *Down in Our Village* is dated 1857 — but only three or four were produced, none with any great success.[2] In 1860, the year his infant daughter died, he decided to abandon the theatrical world and turned instead to journalism, drama criticism, and fiction writing. This letter shows that Robertson intended to make his career change permanent and felt extremely bitter toward the theatre just two years before his success began with *David Garrick* in 1864 and continued with his six major comedies — *Society, Ours, Caste, Play, School,* and *M.P.* — at the Prince of Wales's Theatre.

As a journalist who contributed to many periodicals, Robertson often drummed up his own business. On 18 or 19 June 1862[3] he wrote to an old friend (name unknown) living in Grantham to ask if any of the local papers needed a London correspondent to report weekly on political, literary, and social events. As if to establish his credentials, Robertson declared:

> *I am now connected with newspapers and am not only a journalist but an author generally — and I am happy as well as astonished to say that I have no reason to grumble at my success in my new position. I have been and am still doing well — in fact I have been singularly fortunate since I first started.*

This statement may contain more wishful thinking than truth. A year later Henry Vizetelly, founding editor of the *Illustrated Times*, commissioned a series of articles from Robertson ("a youngish-looking fellow, whose shabby attire and careworn, dejected expression conveyed the idea that he was not of the fortunate ones of this world") and noted his "anxious, pleading look" and "doleful countenance."[4]

Daniel Barrett is Adjunct Assistant Professor in the Department of English at Iowa State University.

Whatever his professional fortunes might have been, Robertson was apparently unlucky in love. Since he had not seen his Grantham friend for about fifteen years, Robertson informed him that he had married and fathered three children, two of whom survived. Then, in a remarkably frank admission considering he was not on intimate terms with his correspondent, he added:

> *It is so common a thing for poor people to increase their responsibilities under the sentimental hope of lightening or sharing their burthens, that I need hardly tell you that I was not prudent enough to seek a partner with any present or expected means of helping me.*

This confession helps to explain Robertson's strangely ambivalent attitude toward marriage in his plays. Typically the obligatory happy ending in Victorian comedy called for an engagement or imminent marriage. Yet Robertson, while following this general formula, enjoyed puncturing the ideal of wedded bliss with some of his most pointed dialogue. According to Hugh Chalcot in *Ours,* a character who in some respects resembles the author, "Marriage is a mistake, but ready money's real enjoyment." When someone says of the soldiers departing for the Crimean War, "Poor fellows — leaving their wives!" Chalcot responds, "They consider that one of the privileges of the profession."[5] Such observations, innocent as they might seem, exposed Robertson to frequent charges of cynicism and pessimism, yet in subsequent plays he refused to alter his opinion to suit the public's sensitive tastes.

The most surprising revelation in the letter, however, is Robertson's unbridled contempt for the theatre:

> *Since I used to correct the playbills for the Grantham Theatre — a magnificent and palatial Institution now happily fallen into decay, and as I hear, converted into a Methodist chapel [—] I have abandoned my former unremunerative and nomadic calling and now hate theatricals and all things thereunto pertaining with a hearty intensity only to be appreciated by those who have been connected with that dreadful business and unsuccessful in its pursuit.*

We have long known that Robertson resented the lack of encouragement he had received in his acting and playwriting. At his clubs and at dinner parties with friends he often berated theatre managers in particular for their stinginess, adherence to tradition, and neglect of talented but obscure writers.[6] What is most surprising here is the vehemence of Robertson's scorn and the determination to forsake the theatre permanently. The long-accepted view of Robertson as the dedicated reformer patiently waiting for his day to arrive, the basis of Tom Wrench in *Trelawny of the "Wells,"* simply does not hold up.

Is there a possibility that Robertson intentionally exaggerated his contempt for the theatre? I can think of only two reasons for such a ruse: (1) He wanted to convince his friend that he had indeed left the theatre forever and would remain steadfast in his new occupation. But such a scathing denunciation was unnecessary for this purpose; Robertson seems more self-indulgent than self-conscious here. (2) His friend harbored an anti-theatrical prejudice, common enough at that time, which Robertson was trying to exploit. However, it is unlikely that a friendship would have ever developed between one who loathed the theatre and one whose whole life was the theatre, especially since Robertson must have met his friend when the Lincoln troupe performed at Grantham, a regular stop on the circuit. Robertson's bitterness seems sincere, which makes it extremely fortuitous that he ever wrote another play after *The Cantab*, produced in 1861. If not for the intercession of E. A. Sothern, the popular comedian who promoted *David Garrick* as a personal acting vehicle, one of the most respected and influential Victorian dramatists might well have remained silent, seriously retarding the development of original English comedy in the late nineteenth century.

## NOTES

[1]The letter and play are catalogued together as M154/1/5 Theatre Collection #2 in the Department of Special Collections. I am grateful to Barbara Begley, Library Specialist, for her help in locating this letter.

[2]See Daniel Barrett, "T. W. Robertson's Plays: Revisions to Nicoll's Handlist," forthcoming in *Nineteenth Century Theatre Research*, 11 (1983).

[3]Although the year does not appear in the letter, Robertson mentions the possibility of his friend's visiting the "confusing Exhibition" of 1862, open in London from 1 May to 1 November.

[4]Henry Vizetelly, *Glances Back Through Seventy Years* (London, 1893), II, 120-21.

[5]Quoted from *Principal Dramatic Works of Thomas William Robertson* (London, 1889), II, 433, 458.

[6]John Coleman, *Players and Playwrights I Have Known* (London, 1888), II, 158; Clement Scott, *The Drama of Yesterday and To-day* (London, 1899), I, 481; Sir Francis C. Burnand, *Records and Reminiscences* (London, 1904), II, 53.

# Feature Section: Theatre History Obscurities

Theatre History Obscurities will feature the visual reproduction of a wide variety of theatre related items from libraries, institutes, museums, and private collections that have not previously been published or are not readily available.

## Part I: The Roman Amphitheatre in Alexandria, Egypt

## Part II: Theatrical Contracts and Letterheads

## Part I: The Roman Amphitheatre in Alexandria, Egypt

In 1964 while digging the foundation for a new high rise building in the center of Alexandria, Roman columns were unearthed. The columns were part of a Roman Amphitheatre structure which was subsequently researched and excavated by the Polish Expedition of Kazimierz Michalowski in the area known as Kom el Dekka. The site is near the main railroad station in the center of the city, not far from erroneously named Pompey's Pillar (actually Roman prefect Posthumus's tribute to Emperor Diocletian) and, almost as if planned, directly behind the Greco-Roman Museum founded in 1891.

The Amphitheatre is actually an odeum (Greek — odeion) that was used for music concerts, recitations, symposia, and other intellectual stimulation. The excavation of this odeum is important not only because it is extremely well preserved and the only one to be discovered in Egypt, but significant because the Romans did not build many odea. Only one is known to have been constructed in Rome. Usually the Romans built odea near larger amphitheatres and many odea were eventually converted into arenas for gladiator competition, etc. The most well known odeum is the one built by Herodes Atticus in Athens. Other fine examples of odea are located in Pompeii, Taormina, Corinth, Burtrinto in Albania, etc. A unique feature of the odeum is the vaulted roof covering the structure, consequently the often horseshoe shaped orchestra and smaller seating capacity. The Alexandria structure will seat approximately 800 persons. The Michalowski Expedition substantially corroborates their supposition that the theatre had a vaulted roof at one time. A variety of cross elements in decoration and numerous construction elements uncovered during the excavation suggest that the function of the theatre changed over several centuries. The original structure probably dates from the early first century A.D. Many Greek inscriptions concerning horse races were found in the house of the theatre and one arabic inscription on a pedestal in the back stage area originates from the Omayyad period (658-968). Early Christian symbols carved in stone are also to be found.

Excavation of the entire area surrounding the Amphitheatre is still in progress. The news of this discovery has been overshadowed, no doubt, by recent events in Egyptian archeology, e.g., the X-raying of various Egyptian antiquities, etc. The Polish Center for Egyptian Archeology is expected to publish extensive information concerning the excavation of the site.

For general information on odea see Margarete Bieber, *The History of the Greek and Roman Theatre*, 2nd ed. (Princeton, N.Y.: Princeton Univ. Press, 1961), pp. 174-176, 220-222., and James H. Butler, *The Theatre and Drama of Greece and Rome* (San Francisco: Chandler Publishing, 1972), pp. 92-94. For **new** and many old photographs of Roman Amphitheatres on over 150 black and white glossy plates see Rainer Graefe, *Vela Erunt, die Zeltdaecher der roemischen Theater und aehnlicher Anlagen*, 2 vols. (Mainz: Verlag Philipp von Zabern, 1979). For specific information on the Michalowski Expedition see Irena Pomorska, "Polish Excavations in Egypt and Sudan 1964-65", *Africana Bulletin* (Warsaw), 4 (1966), 108-116.

Ron Engle

# Part I: The Roman Amphitheatre in Alexandria, Egypt

General view of the Roman Amphitheatre discovered in 1964 and excavated by the Polish Expedition of Kazimierz Michalowski at Kom el Dekka in the center of Alexandria, Egypt. The site is conveniently near the Greco-Roman Museum. Photo courtesy the Department of Tourism, Arab Republic of Egypt.

Back view of the Amphitheatre revealing fragments of the vault and reinforcements presumably used for a roof support structure. The Amphitheatre was actually an odeum. Photographed by Ron Engle, 1978.

A view of the orchestra area. Photo, Ron Engle, 1978.

A view of the cavea from the stage area. Twelve marble tiers provide seating for approximately 800 people. Photo, Ron Engle, 1978.

A view from the cavea looking toward the stage showing the extension of the seating beyond the left aisle where a parados would normally be located. Photo, Ron Engle, 1978.

The support sub-structure between the vestibule and the inner wall reinforcements. Photo, Ron Engle, 1978.

Columns made of marble and colored granite formed a columnade for the cavea. Photo, Ron Engle, 1978.

Two views of the stage and remains of the scaenae frons from the cavea. Photo, Ron Engle, 1978.

# Part II: Theatrical Contracts and Letterheads

The Metropolitan Opera House in Grand Forks, N.D., photographed for a postcard in 1910. The Opera House was opened on November 10, 1890 at a cost of $91,000 with a seating capacity of 900. The backstage area was seventy-five feet wide and thirty-two feet deep. Painted drops, wings, and flats were supplied by Peter Clausen of Minneapolis and included the standard: perspective street, horizon, landscape garden, cut wood, rocky pass, landscape, kitchen doors, plain chamber doors, fancy center door, king's palace, gothic chamber, prison doors, and dark wood. The drop curtain, border, flats and wings were painted on Emerald canvas and the drops, set pieces, sky, wood and drapery borders on cotton cloth. There were six dressing rooms and a chorus dressing room. The fly loft, box office and orchestra pit were connected with speaking tubes. Summer air conditioning was supplied by air passing through an ice chamber. The Opera House attracted many productions from the main northern circuit from Minneapolis-St. Paul to Seattle and served as a stopover enroute to profitable Winnipeg in Canada. For a time it was a major link in the Red River Valley Circuit of Brainard, Crookston, Fargo, Winnipeg, and Grand Forks. In the above photograph the poster bill on the right announces the appearance of Viola Allen accompanied by James O'Neill, Minna Gale and Henry Stanford in *The White Sister* by F. Marion Crawford (Liebler & Co. Managers). For this production top admission price was raised from $1.50 to $2.00. In 1940 the fly loft and stage were razed and the remaining structure is now a bowling alley, bar, etc. Original postcard in the private collection of Ron Engle. Original building plans, inventory records, etc., in the Orin G. Libby Manuscript Collection, Chester Fritz Library, University of North Dakota, Grand Forks, N.D.

SEASON OF 91-92.

C. H. Truesdell

In the Grand Russian Military and Comedy Drama

MICHAEL STROGOFF

SUPPORTED BY A
SUPERB COMPANY

In a carefully selected repertoire of NEW YORK MELODRAMATIC and COMEDY SUCCESSES
Under the Personal Management of

J. B. HARDEBECK.

**To Managers:**

Knowing the long felt wants of managers and the public, we have decided to place a

THOROUGHLY EQUIPPED COMPANY

of artists before the people in a Repertoire of

SPECIAL COMEDIES

and MELODRAMAS

—INCLUDING—

"MICHAEL STROGOFF,"
"INSIDE TRACK"
*(By permission of Oliver Doud Byron).*

The New Military Drama,

"Army Portia,"

and others, ALL well known and ALL New York successes.

We have the right to play ALL of our pieces, as we pay royalties for them.

We carry the finest company that can be selected from the host of road people in New York.

\+ + +

OUR PRINTING

is all of the finest and special. We can give you from three to five hundred sheets, and NOT a duplicate sheet.

\+ + +

Our Special Scenery

is all new, and from the artistic brush of Martini.

\+ + +

OUR CALCIUM EFFECTS

are the sole property of C. H. Truesdell, being invented by him.

*Truly yours,*

HARDEBECK & TRUESDELL.

Saint Cloud Minn

Oct 6th 1891

~~Geo. H. Broadhurst~~
Grand Forks N. D.

Dear Sir :- The Twin Cities Dailies have informed you before this time, no doubt, of the result of misplaced confidence in my former business associate C. H. Truesdell. Owing to his actions and for various other reasons I have concluded to cancel all dates, and close my company. You will therefore be kind enough to cancel our engagement in your city Viz :- Nov 2nd to 7th inclusive. See the N. Y. Clipper of last week regarding C. H. Truesdell

Yours Truly
J B Hardebeck

This letter from J. B. Hardebeck in 1891 to the manager of the Metropolitan Opera House in Grand Forks, George Broadhurst, requests cancellation of their engagement "owing to the actions" and "misplaced confidence in my former business associate C. H. Truesdell." According to the *New York Clipper* of 3 October 1891 the treasurer of the Chicago Haymarket, George A. Fair, refused the "courtesies" of that theatre to C.H. Truesdell, upon which Truesdell threatened to "roast the Haymarket in *The Clipper*." The editor assures Mr. Fair that the paper does not "satisfy" private grudges. "Does any professional, indeed, need to be told that much?" Original letter in the Orin G. Libby Manuscript Collection, E. J. Lander Papers, Chester Fritz Library, University of North Dakota.

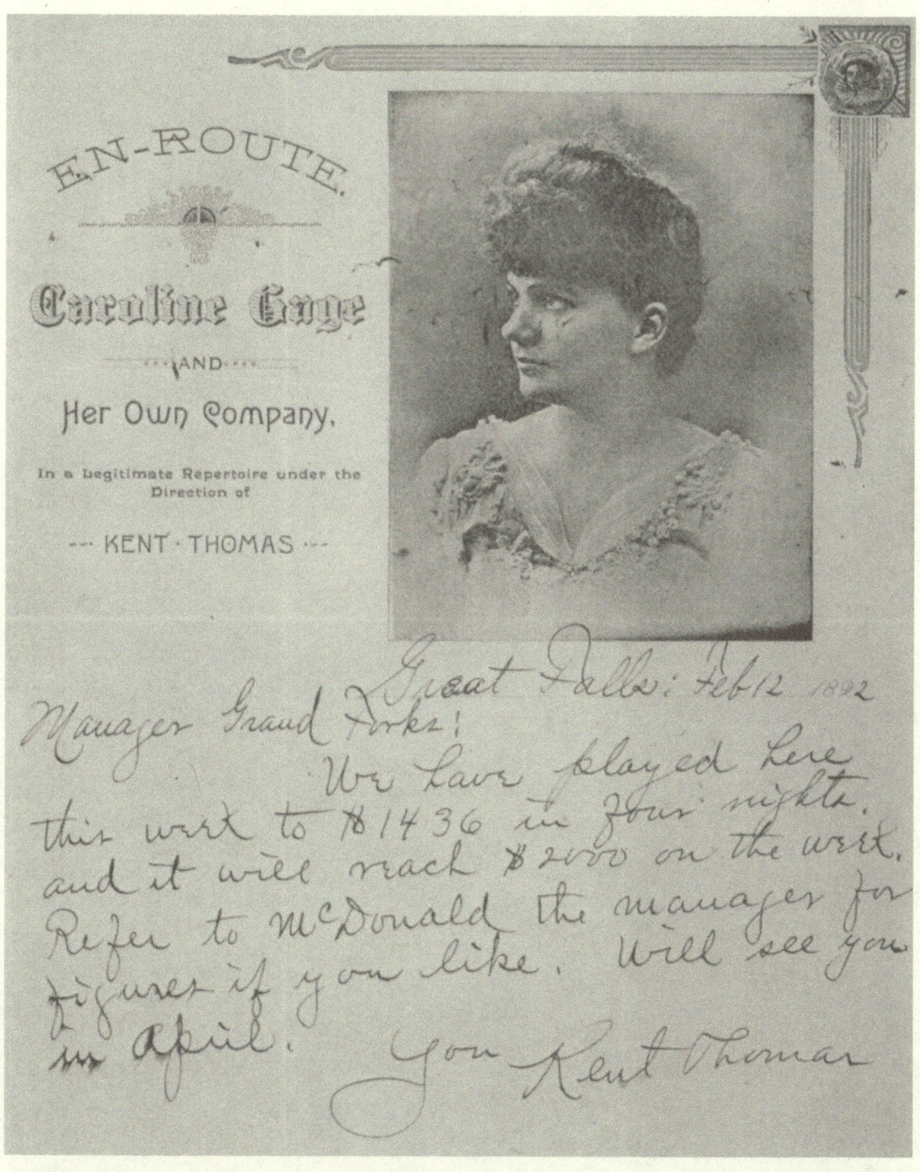

EN-ROUTE.

Caroline Gage

AND

Her Own Company.

In a Legitimate Repertoire under the Direction of

KENT THOMAS

Great Falls: Feb 12 1892

Manager Grand Forks!

We have played here this week to $1436 in four nights. and it will reach $2000 on the week. Refer to McDonald the manager for figures if you like. Will see you in April.

Your Kent Thomas

This letter written from Great Falls, Montana in February of 1982 by Caroline Gage's manager Kent Thomas, boasts $1,436 in receipts for four nights; an enticement to manager Frank Witt of the Metropolitan Opera House in Grand Forks for Gage's April engagement. Caroline Gage and "Her Own Company" performed *The Honey Moon* (4-4-1892), *Pygmalion and Galatea* (4-5-1892), and *Oliver Twist* (4-6-1892). Original letter in the Orin G. Libby Manuscript Collection, E. J. Lander Papers, Chester Fritz Library, University of North Dakota.

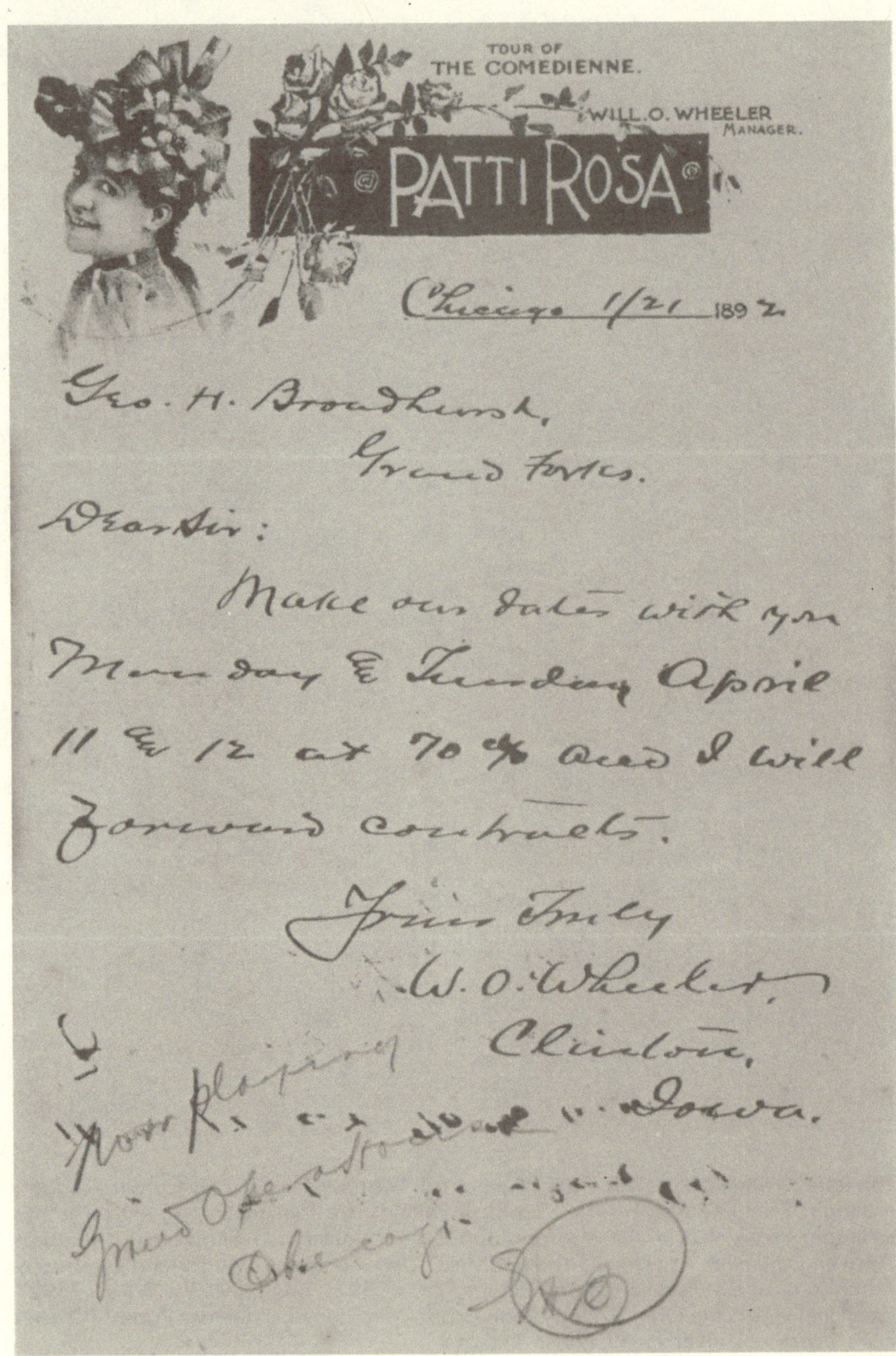

TOUR OF
THE COMEDIENNE.
PATTI ROSA
WILL. O. WHEELER
MANAGER.

Chicago 1/21 1892.

Geo. H. Broadhurst,
Grand Forks.

Dear Sir:

Make our dates with you Monday & Tuesday April 11 & 12 at 70 % and I will forward contracts.

Yours Truly
W. O. Wheeler.
Clinton,
Iowa.

Now playing
Grand Opera House
Chicago

This letter from Will. O. Wheeler written in Chicago in January of 1892 to George Broadhurst (Frank Witt was manager at the time) of the Metropolitan Opera House in Grand Forks, confirms Patti Rosa's engagement for 11 and 12 April for "70%" of the gross receipts. Sixty-five and seventy percent were typical percentages issued by this theatre. Patti Rosa and Co. actually performed on 12 April only, in one of her most popular successes *Dolly Varden* by Charles T. Vincent. Supporting cast members included Will Mandeville, Joe Cawthrone, Grace Gaylor Clark, Charles A. Gardner, Gerald Griffin, and John W. Dunne, her husband. Incidental to the play Rosa introduced medleys, trios, banjo solos, etc., and her "great winking song" *Over the High Brick Wall*. The New York *Dramatic Mirror* 14 February 1891 reported the "little star captured Los Angeles bodily" and in Arizona and Southern California "it was simply a matter of how many tickets should be sold before refusing money." On 9 January 1892 publicity in the *Dramatic Mirror* informs us that the company observed Christmas in Dallas, Texas. The Dallas Lodge of Elks sent Miss Rosa a "writing set of silver." Dunne gave her a diamond and turquoise ring and manager Will. O. Wheeler received a gold-mounted umbrella inscribed "W.O.W., from Patti Rosa." From *The Spirit of the Times* (New York) 11 December 1894 we learn of her untimely death at the age of thirty from the effects of an operation for appendicitis. "A bright, pleasant, little actress, she will be missed. . . ." Original letter in the Orin G. Libby Manuscript Collection, E.J. Lander Papers, Chester Fritz Library, University of North Dakota.

GRAND OPERA HOUSE

LOUIS J. COLUMBUS

FRANK E. ARNOLD

ACTUAL COST.

$50,000

As Complete as
MONEY AND MODERN ART
Can Make It.

The Only Theatre in the City.

Drawing Population, 22,000.

SEATING CAPACITY.

800

PROMENADE FOYER.

Heated by Steam,
Lighted Throughout
By Electricity.

Dressing Rooms on Stage Floor.

SIZE OF STAGE.

27 X 60 FEET

Extra Good Fire Protection.

All of the Latest Appliances and Equipments.

Twelve Complete Sets of Scenery.

CAN PROPERLY STAGE THE LARGEST

Spectacular Productions
On the Road.

CROOKSTON is situated on the Great Northern and Northern Pacific Railways and in the very heart of the largest and best wheat growing region in the world. It is 26 miles from Grand Forks, 65 miles from Fargo and Moorhead, and 125 from Winnipeg. Best of hotel accommodations, 2 daily and 4 weekly newspapers.

Address all communications to
COLUMBUS & ARNOLD, Mgrs.
Lock Box 734, Crookston, Minn.

P. S.—The people of this town wear clothes and shoes and also eat occasionally.

Crookston, Minn., Mch 21 1892

John S. Bucholz Esq.
Grand Forks N. D.

Dear Sir,—

I understand the Manager of your Opera House is about to leave you, and that you want a new manager, or lease.

If such is the case, would there be any prospect for my obtaining it, providing we can come to satisfactory terms? An early reply would oblige.

Yours Very Truly,
L. J. Columbus

The Grand Opera House in Crookston, Minnesota, twenty-six miles from the Metropolitan Opera House in Grand Forks, N.D., was built in 1890. The letterhead provides the "details". The Theatre became part of the Red River Valley Circuit, which included Brainard, Fargo, Grand Forks, and Winnipeg in Canada. In this letter written in March of 1982, manager Louis J. Columbus (pictured in the upper left corner of the letterhead) is applying for the position of manager at the Metropolitan Opera House in Grand Forks, N.D. Mr. Columbus was not hired. Note the "P.S." in the bottom left corner. Original letter in the Orin G. Libby Manuscript Collection, E. J. Lander Papers, Chester Fritz Library, University of North Dakota.

·1893· "ON·EARTH·THERE·NEVER·WAS·ITS·LIKE." ·1894·

SUTTON'S

·MONSTER SPECTACULAR DOUBLE·

UNCLE TOM'S CABIN COMPANY AND SPECIALTY ANNEX·

2 COMPLETE·SHOWS 2

·TRAVELING·IN·THEIR·OWN·TRAIN·OF·VESTIBULE·PALACE·CARS·

·THE·STRONGEST·MATINEE·ATTRACTION·IN·AMERICA·

DICK P. SUTTON Manager. R. A. GRAHAM BUSINESS REPRESENTATIVE

"TRUTH·SACRED·TRUTH·"
"ALWAYS THE LARGEST"
"SURELY·THE·BEST·OF·ALL"
"PARADE·THE·FINEST·AND·GRANDEST"
"THE·LEADING·UNCLE·TOM·SHOW"
"PLAYING·TO·THE·LARGEST·BUSINESS"
"THE·SHOW·THAT·MANAGERS·WANT"
"BAND & ORCHESTRA·SIMPLY·IN·IT"
"WARDROBE & UNIFORMS·ELEGANT"
"SCENERY·ABUNDANT & TRUE·TO·NATURE"
"HERALDED·WITH·ENTHUSIASM"
"POSITIVELY·BETTER·THIS SEASON·THAN·EVER·BEFORE"
"CAPABLE·LADIES·AND·GENTLEMEN·IN·THE·CAST"
"BOOK·US·IF·YOU·CAN"
"WE·WANT·TO·DO·'BIZ'·WITH·YOU"
"ADVANCED·WITH·ALL·THE·BEST·PRINTING & NOVEL·IDEAS·IN·THE·ADVERTISING·WORLD"

Dickinson Nov 26 1893

Mr Lander Dr Sir I met a Gentleman
Friend of yours & Explained a little
business Matter Concerning the Opera
House at your City. He tells me if I
would write you that I would get an
answer also that you would see me
righted. I played a date at that House
Shortly & as I did not have a contract
with me & the Gentleman I settled with
had none we settled at 65–35 When
I got down my Car I discovered the mistake
I sent wife back to theatre at once & ~~she~~
Seen the manager He said Mrs
Sutton I know they settled wrong
with Mr Sutton but our treasurer
is gone home ~~but~~ tell Mr Sutton that
I will bring Him His money down
in the Morning. Well He lied He
did not do it. I wrote Him 2 letters
And I telegraphed to Him to send
my Money He was not man
Enough to even reply or send the
Money. There is 12 27 Coming to me
honestly from that House & to be
treated as I was by Him and
believing that He has that money

The letterhead of Sutton's *Uncle Tom's Cabin* Company illustrates the "puffing" of Sutton's publicity. Sutton's production featured "2 Famous Topsies, 2 Marks, the Lawyers, 2 Educated Donkeys, 4 Cuban Bloodhounds, and 4 Shetland Ponies." Maude Sutton was billed as the youngest Topsy on the stage. "Baby Edith," five years old, appeared as the Angel Child. The company also featured a quartet of colored singers. The parade was held the day of the performance 31 October 1893. The *Grand Forks Herald* of 1 November 1893 reported that attendance was "fair" for that kind of show. The production was "so cut up with specialties that it was difficult at times to recognize it." The reporter did praise however, the colored singing as a pleasing feature. Tickets were priced 25¢, 50¢, and 75¢. The content of

·1893· "ON · EARTH · THERE · NEVER · WAS · ITS · LIKE" ·1894·

SUTTON'S

·MONSTER SPECTACULAR DOUBLE·

UNCLE TOM'S CABIN COMPANY AND SPECIALTY ANNEX·

2 COMPLETE · SHOWS 2

·TRAVELING · IN · THEIR · OWN · TRAIN · OF · VESTIBULE · PALACE · CARS·

·THE · STRONGEST · MATINEE · ATTRACTION · IN · AMERICA·

DICK P. SUTTON Manager. R. A. GRAHAM BUSINESS REPRESENTATIVE

TRUTH · SACRED · TRUTH ·
"ALWAYS THE LARGEST"
"SURELY · THE · BEST · OF · ALL"
"PARADE · THE · FINEST · AND · GRANDEST"
"THE · LEADING · UNCLE · TOM · SHOW"
"PLAYING · TO THE · LARGEST · BUSINESS"
"THE · SHOW · THAT · MANAGERS · WANT"
"BAND & ORCHESTRA · SIMPLY · IN · IT"
"WARDROBE & UNIFORMS ELEGANT"
"SCENERY · ABUNDANT · & TRUE · TO · NATURE"
"HERALDED · WITH · ENTHUSIASM"
"POSITIVELY · BETTER · THIS SEASON · THAN · EVER · BEFORE"
"CAPABLE · LADIES · AND GENTLEMEN · IN · THE · CAST"
"BOOK · US · IF · YOU · CAN"
"WE · WANT · TO · DO · BIZ · WITH · YOU"
"ADVANCED · WITH · ALL · THE · BEST · PRINTING & NOVEL · IDEAS · IN · THE · ADVERTISING · WORLD"

2 ______________ 189_

as why I write you this letter
I am not hard up for the amount
I have Considerable show Property & I
Am well Known in the Biz I have
never had an insult like this
before so if you will get me
7 06 Dollars and send to me I
buy you a Hat with the other
Five I will tell letter or give
the Entire amount to some poor
needy woman I would rather
do that than have it go over
the River in Saloons He told me
that He was going with the
Ringling Brothers Circus next
Year well you may tell Him
for me that He will Never
stay long unless He sends me
my MONEY Hoping you will
drop me a line in the Enclosed
Envelope Truly yours

Dick P. Sutton

the above letter written by Dick Sutton to E. J. Lander, lawyer manager for the Metropolitan Opera House, concerns a small amount of money, $12.27, which Sutton claims was owed him. He stakes his reputation on the line and offers to buy Lander a hat and give the rest of the money to "some poor needy women." "I would rather do that than have it go over the river in saloons." This is a reference to the thriving saloon business at the time (thirty-two in all) in East Grand Forks, Minnesota, across the Red River from the Metropolitan Opera House in Grand Forks, N.D. Original letter in the Orin G. Libby Manuscript Collection, E. J. Lander Papers, Chester Fritz Library, University of North Dakota.

The back side of Sutton's stationary depicting the parade and his "vestibule palace cars."

**CHARLES FROHMAN,**
EMPIRE THEATRE BUILDING,
BROADWAY AND 40TH STREET.
REPRESENTING PRINCIPAL THEATRES AND ATTRACTIONS.

**BOOKING + DEPARTMENT,**
JULIUS CAHN, Manager.

ALWAYS ON TOUR THROUGHOUT THE REGULAR SEASON FROM FIFTEEN TO TWENTY LEADING COMPANIES IN THE LEADING SUCCESSES.

## SHARING CONTRACT.

**This Agreement,** Made and entered into this 14th day of July 1898 between Julius Cahn party of the first part, and E. J. Lander party of the second part,

**Witnesseth,** That the said party of the second part, in consideration of one dollar, the receipt of which is hereby acknowledged, agrees to play the party of the first part in Grand Forks N. Dak. a period of 1 night ~~and~~ ~~usual matinee~~, commencing Feb. 23 1899 and agrees to furnish in this contract the Metropolitan Theatre well lighted, cleaned and heated, with all the requisite attachés, both in rear and before the curtain included; ~~organ and piano on stage~~; necessary stage hands; orchestra; all licenses; scenery and equipments in theatre; house programmes; coupon tickets; all bill-posting; bill boards; distributing and hanging; and advertise usual squares one week in advance of opening in each issue of each local paper, and to continue same throughout the entire engagement, and to receive all baggage, scenery and properties on the arrival of the company, at the stage door, and to carefully carry the same to all dressing and property rooms and stage; and to take the same from dressing and property rooms and stage and deliver outside of stage door immediately after last performance ending same engagement, FREE.

The party of the first part agrees to furnish in this contract The Girl I Left Behind Me to furnish all transportation, express, freight and baggage charges for its company, and advance printing, lithographs, etc.

In consideration of which the party of the first part, viz., Julius Cahn is to receive 70 per cent. of the gross receipts of each and every performance

The party of the first part reserves the right to furnish all tickets and pass-out checks if he so desires.
~~The party of the first part reserves the right to regulate the~~ prices during this engagement to be regular house prices.
The regular officers of the house are to have control of the doors and box-office, under the supervision of both parties to this contract, who are to have free access to the box-office at all times.
A settlement is to be made every performance both from the ticket-seller's statement, which is to be furnished previous to counting the boxes, and the box count.
It is further understood and agreed, that if by reason of sickness or accident, or from any other unforeseen event, the parties of the first part are not able to meet this engagement, they shall not be held liable for any damages of any name or nature.

**Witness** our hands and seals the day and year first above written.

Julius Cahn Mgr. [L. S.]

[L. S.]

If terms of this contract are not satisfactory please return without erasure.

A standard Charles Frohman "Sharing Contract" booking *The Girl I Left Behind Me* at seventy percent of the gross receipts for 23 February 1899 in the Metropolitan Opera House in Grand Forks, N.D. Original contract in the Orin G. Libby Manuscript Collection, E. J. Lander Papers, Chester Fritz Library, University of North Dakota.

PRIMROSE & DOCKSTADER'S

GEO. PRIMROSE

Greater

American

Minstrels

Primrose & Dockstader,
Proprietors.

JAS. H. DECKER
Manager

LEW. DOCKSTADER

This Agreement, Made this 22nd day of July A. D. 1898, between E.J. Lander of Grand Forks, N.D. and JAMES H. DECKER, Manager of PRIMROSE & DOCKSTADER'S MINSTRELS, contracting to play Primrose & Dockstader's Minstrels at Metropolitan Theatre, Grand Forks, N.D.- Wednesday, May 10th, 1899.

Said E.J. Lander

A Primrose and Dockstader's Greater American Minstrels contract made out in July 1898 for a 10 May 1899 performance at the Metropolitan Opera House in Grand Forks, N.D. Note the standard performance exclusion for other Minstrels and the specific exclusion of the Wilson and Cleveland's Minstrels for nearly one full year.

to furnish said Metropolitan Theatre License, Stage Men, Ushers, Stage Furniture, Bill Posting, Bill Boards and Distributing. ~~Regular Three Sheet Posters~~, Newspaper Advertisements in all daily and Sunday papers one week in advance. Properties, assist in placing baggage in and out of building and dressing rooms, a sufficient number of round back chairs for first part setting. Ticket Sellers, Special Police, House Programmes, Coupon Tickets, Advance Sales, and also agrees to post all advance stands and printing one week previous to regular billing. Said E.J. Lander also agrees not to play or rent any other Minstrel Company at prices less than 25 cents to one dollar, prior to above Company's appearance. No other performance of any character whatever to be given in said theatre on above date. No other Minstrels to perform in said Metropolitan Theatre within three weeks prior to above date, and 2 weeks after the same.

If above condition of this agreement is violated, said PRIMROSE & DOCKSTADER to receive ten (10) per cent. additional of the gross receipts.

Said JAMES H. DECKER to furnish PRIMROSE & DOCKSTADER MINSTREL COMPANY, including Brass Band and Orchestra and entertainment complete, in a first-class and commendable shape; with door tenders, admission tickets, free list tickets, and printing necessary for the proper advertisement of the entertainment.

No cash to be advanced or loaned to any agent or member of above Company unless the same is authorized by PRIMROSE & DOCKSTADER.

Said PRIMROSE & DOCKSTADER to receive (75 per cent. of the gross receipts.

Said E.J. Lander to receive (25 per cent. of the gross receipts.

Said E.J. Lander agrees not to play or rent the Wilson & Cleveland's Minstrels prior to the appearance of the above company in said theatre.

~~or £ certainty per night~~, with settlement at each performance. Box Office statement to be rendered before counting ticket boxes, and controlled by tickets received at Doors. ~~No free tickets issued except to the Press.~~ Free-list mutual.

If from any unforseen event, national calamity, action of the elements or any other reason, PRIMROSE & DOCKSTADER should fail to fulfill above agreement, they are not to be liable for any damage whatever.

If terms of this Contract are not satisfactory, please return without alterations or erasures.

J H Decker

The competition was close on their heels. The Metropolitan booked Hi-Henry's Minstrels for 19 April 1899, exactly three weeks prior to Primrose and Dockstader as specified in the contract. Original contract in the Orin G. Libby Manuscript Collection, E. J. Lander Papers, Chester Fritz Library, University of North Dakota.

# O'NEIL & MASTERS' "HUMANITY" COMPANY.

## SHARING CONTRACT.

This Agreement, Made and entered into this 13th day of Aug 1898, between O'NEIL & MASTERS, Managers, party of the first part, and ~~C.P. Walker~~ E. J. Lander party of the second part.

Witnesseth, That the said party of the second part, in consideration of one dollar, the receipt of which is hereby acknowledged, agrees to play the party of the first part in the city of Grand Forks N.D. a period of one nights and — ~~matinee~~, commencing Feby 16 1899, and agrees to furnish in this contract the Metropolitan Theater well lighted, cleaned and heated, with all the requisite attaches, both in rear and before the curtain, included; necessary stage hands; full orchestra; all licenses; stage furniture; ~~piano for use upon the stage~~; ~~calcium lights~~; imperishable properties; scenery; tackle and ropes for drops, and equipments in accordance with the plots furnished; ~~regular three sheet posters~~, house programmes; coupon tickets; all bill posting; bill boards; distributing and hanging; and advertise usual squares one week in advance of opening in each issue of each local paper, and to continue the same throughout the entire engagement; and to receive all baggage, scenery and properties, on the arrival of the company, at the stage door, and to carefully carry the same to all dressing and property rooms and stage, and to take the same from dressing and property rooms and stage, and deliver outside of stage door immediately after last performance; the theatre to be kept open and lighted for the removal of the company's scenery and baggage, ending same engagement, FREE.

The party of the first part agrees to furnish in this contract Humanity Co and furnish all transportation, express, freight and baggage charges for its company, and advance printing, lithographs, etc.

In consideration of which the party of the first part, viz.: O'NEIL & MASTERS, or their representative, is to receive Seventy per cent. of the gross receipts of each and every performance.

Regular prices (25, 50, 75, & 1.00) agreed upon

~~The party of the first part reserves the right to regulate the prices and furnish all tickets and pass-out checks if they so desire.~~

The party of the first part to have the privilege of furnishing the supers used in this production either from the audience or the street, at their option, ~~and they shall also have the sole and exclusive privilege of selling books and pictures in the Theatre Lobby and in the Front of the House~~.

It is further agreed that during this engagement no performance or rehearsal other than herein stipulated shall take place at the above-mentioned building without the consent of the said first party.

A settlement is to be made both from the ticket sellers' statement (which is to be furnished previous to counting the boxes) and the box count.

It is also agreed that free admissions shall be mutual, and under no circumstances are "clipped" or season tickets admissible.

In consideration of this agreement the party of the second part hereby agrees that under no circumstances whatever will he permit any piratical version (or anything bearing any semblance to the same) of this, or any attraction under the control of O'NEIL & MASTERS.

The party of the first part is in no way responsible for any moneys advanced to their agent or representative unless specially authorized in writing.

This contract is a personal contract and not assignable, and must be carried out by the parties hereto and not by others.

The fulfillment of this contract is settlement in full of all demands of whatsoever nature or kind against the party of the first part.

The party of the first part is not to be held responsible in case sickness, war, riot, or any other unforeseen occurrence should prevent them filling above date, ~~and hereby reserve the right to cancel this agreement at any time upon giving two weeks' notice (in writing) of such intention~~.

All contracts made previous to this date to be considered null and void.

*Witness* our hands and seals the day and year first above written.

O'Neal & Masters per H.D.

E. J. Lander per C.P. Walker L.S.

N.B.— If any clause in this contract is objectionable to the party of the second part, it should be returned without alteration, with a letter stating objections. ***Please do not alter, erase or interline.*** – O'N & M.

A standard O'Neil and Masters' "Humanity" Company "Sharing Contract" made out for seventy percent of the gross receipts for a performance on 16 February 1899. Original contract in the Orin G. Libby Manuscript Collection, E. J. Lander Papers, Chester Fritz Library, University of North Dakota.

# Theatre History Crossword Puzzle II

**FELICIA HARDISON LONDRÉ**

## CLUES

ACROSS

1. Site of retheatricalization
11. He wrote for Bracegirdle.
12. Missouri ______________ Theatre
17. Yefremov's first name
18. "Off" in London
19. Reverse initials of author of *Remote Control* (1929)
20. Ballroom theatre in Vienna
21. Grown-up baby in *The Late Christopher Bean*
23. Polish Madame
28. Babies on Broadway
29. Actress Marie ______________ (1882-1956)
30. How seventeenth-century actors split the take to buy their suppers (Fr.)
32. ___________ Wallach
33. Popular American author of light farces in early 1900s
35. San Francisco company
36. Who married an angel in 1938
37. *Papa — All*
38. What Tairov left behind
39. Tammaso Salvi--
43. When Sarah Bernhardt did her farewell tour of America
45. Wrote a slum play for Mrs. Fiske
48. Initials of the American hoofer in *Idiot's Delight*
49. First word of play titles by Synge, Brecht, O'Neill, and Augustus Thomas
50. Initials of creator of Mr. Zero
51. RSC's ________________ Place
53. Playmakers' state (Abbrev.)
54. Play by Goldoni
56. Phyllis ---el designed costumes for *Old Bucks and New Wings* (1962)
58. First-name initial and last name of Finnish playwright, author of 1909 historical triology
60. What British actors do between shows
62. Character in *Sodom and Gomorrah*
63. Great classic play for feminists
66. Fr--igan in Arrabal's *Ars amandi*
67. Same as 59 Down
68. ---- *Filii mei* by Arthurius Millerius
69. Artistic Director of the Gorky in Leningrad
70. Initials of dissident Soviet absurdist

DOWN

1. One of the things about theatre that puts you off the most
2. Spanish directress
3. R---cco: style of Cesky Krumlov
4. A role more honored in the breeches than in the observance by Sarah Bernhardt
5. _______________ our Toes
6. Initials of Hell chronicler
7. French movie director (*King of Hearts*)
8. Performer in *Folies Bergère*, a 16-scene vaudeville revue that opened on Broadway December 25, 1939, for example
9. Bernhard's _____________ *of Retirement*
10. What Ethelwold is remembered for
13. Eliza Doolittle's here
14. Euri---es
15. Apostolo Z---
16. Heads of French theatre
19. He visited Hell's Kitchen.
22. Theatre designer whose moustache is more famous than his productions
24. Initials of half of the *Hellzapoppin* creative team

# Theatre History Crossword Puzzle II

**by Felicia Hardison Londré**

25. Expletive in the title of 1965 play
26. Acted role of Cleopatra in his own play about her
27. Charles or Edmund
34. Initials of 45 Across
36. Same as 36 Across
40. Ira Aldridge's great role
41. -- *ne badine pas avec l'amour*
42. Wrote *We Can't Pay? We Won't Pay!*
44. Spencer Golub tells all about him in *Theatre History Studies II*
46. Lane where four theatres have stood
47. MACBETH: I have done the deed. Didst thou not hear a __________?
49. Where Goldoni's mistress worked
52. One who gets slapped
55. Obey's title character (Fr.)
57. Fourth brother in two Broadway hits later made into movies
59. Initials of greatest commedia dell'arte actress
61. Kado Kostzer's latest Paris hit
64. Where "the fiery furnace play" was popular
65. Herne's harbor
66. __________ Claire

The solution will appear in the next issue of *Theatre History Studies*.

## Solution to Theatre History Crossword Puzzle I

| D | R | O | T | T | N | I | N | G | H | O | L | M |
|---|---|---|---|---|---|---|---|---|---|---|---|---|
| E |  | E |  | H | E | R |  | N | O | H |  | O |
| U | R | N |  | E | U | M |  |  | M |  | I | T |
| S | I | S | I |  | B | A | Y | R | E | U | T | H |
| E |  | L | O | V | E |  | E | U |  | M | A | E |
| X |  | A |  | I | R | E | N | E |  |  | L | R |
| M | A | G | I | C |  | N |  | D | O | R | I | C |
| A | P | E |  |  | N | D |  | A |  | M | A | O |
| C | H | R | O | N | E | G | K |  | L |  | N | U |
| H |  |  | N |  | W | A | S |  | A | T |  | R |
| I | R | A | K | E |  | M |  | T | Z | A | R | A |
| N |  | P | O | R | T |  | B | O | Z |  |  | G |
| A | M | B | I | G | U | C | O | M | I | Q | U | E |

# Mid-America Theatre Conference Theatre History Symposium 1983

"Crosscurrents: The Arts of the Theatre" was the theme of the Third Annual Theatre History Symposium of the Mid-America Theatre Conference held at the University of Iowa in Iowa City, March 18-20, 1983. Felicia Hardison Londré, University of Missouri-Kansas City, coordinated the seven-session symposium in which 23 papers explored historical perspectives on the theatre and its relationships to music, painting, film, dance, sculpture, architecture, poetry, and narrative fiction.

Chairing the sessions were: C. J. Gianakaris, Western Michigan University, "Literary and Musical Approaches to Theatre;" Ronald G. Engle, University of North Dakota, "Adaptations of Shakespeare;" Harold J. Nichols, Kansas State University, "The Visual Artist and the Theatre;" Tice L. Miller, University of Nebraska-Lincoln, "Architects and Theatre Architecture;" Felicia Londré, "Poets and Filmmakers in the Theatre;" James S. Moy, University of Wisconsin-Madison, "Post-Modern Performance Art;" and William Kuhlke, University of Kansas, "The Arts of the Russian Theatre"

It was noted that among the impressive number of distinguished scholars participating in the 1983 symposium were editors of six journals: *Comparative Drama, Empirical Research in Theatre, Tennessee Williams Review, Theatre Design and Technology, Theatre History Studies,* and *Theatre Journal*.

The following are the papers presented at the symposium:

Aronson, Arnold: University of Virginia
"Spalding Gray: Performance Artist as Playwright and Actor"
Bank, Rosemarie K.: Lafayette, Indiana
"Theatre and Narrative Fiction in the Work of 19th-Century American Playwright Louisa Medina"
Black, Lendley: Emporia State University
"Artists of the Kamerny Theatre"
Blitgen, Carol: Clark College, Iowa
"Il Teatro Olimpico: Masterpiece of Compromise"
Cima, Gay Gibson: Georgetown University
"The Actor's Art in Creating Pinter's Cinematic *Old Times*"
Deak, Frantisek: University of California, San Diego
"The Art of Personality: Art as a Human Project"
Fantasia, Louis: University of Southern California, Los Angeles
"How the Actors Studio and Cinematic Acting Set Back Theatre in America by a Generation or Two"
Glenn, George D.; University of Northern Iowa
"*The Merry Wives* Operatized"
Golub, Spencer: University of Virginia
"The Difficult Births and Uneasy Deaths of Tadeusz Różewicz"

Gross, Roger: University of Arkansas
"Recovering Shakespeare's Verse Rhythms"
Harris, Laurilyn J.: Washington State University
"Otherwise I Must Have Incumbered the Stage with Dead Bodies: Nahum Tate's *King Lear*"
Jerit, Ron: Jerit/Boys, Inc., Arts Design Consultants, Oak Park, Illinois
"Current Trends in Theatre Architecture"
Lee, Briant Hamor: Bowling Green University
"Architects and Auditoriums of Turn-of-the-19th-Century France and Italy"
Maschio, Geraldine: Iowa State University
"Sources and Resources in the Musical Theatre: The Musical as an Adaptive Art"
Milhous, Judith: University of Iowa
"The Economics of Opera and Theatre in London, 1685-1720"
Nash, Elizabeth H.: University of Minnesota
"Selected Examples of Geraldine Farrar as Actress"
Phillips, Jerrold A.: Northeastern University
"Artistic Styles Reflected in Designs for *The Magic Flute*"
Salter, Denis and Kenneth DeLong: University of Calgary
"C. G. Stanford's Music to Tennyson's *Becket*: A Composer's Interpretation of the Drama"
Schanke, Robert A.: Central College
"Eva LeGallienne: A Servant to Shakespeare"
Vallillo, Stephen M.: New York City
"The Shakespearean Productions of the Federal Theatre Project"
Vince, R. W.: McMaster University, Hamilton, Ontario
"Pageantry and Iconology"
Watt, Stephen: University of Tennessee
"Historical Drama and Historical Painting in Victorian England: The History Plays of Tom Taylor and W. G. Wills"
Witham, Barry: University of Washington
"Performance Art: Implications for Contemporary Theatre"

# Theatre History Symposium 1984

## Shakespearean Production: Acting, Directing and Staging

"Contemporary perspectives on the production of Shakespeare's plays in various languages and/or historical periods" is the theme for the Fourth Annual Theatre History Symposium of the Mid-American Theatre Conference, which will convene in Omaha, Nebraska, on March 16-18, 1984.

Send proposals, outlines, abstracts, or manuscripts by Monday, November 14, 1983 to the Symposium Coordinator: Harold J. Nichols, Department of Speech, Kansas State University, Manhattan, KS 66506;

or to Panel Chairs:

BRITISH PRODUCTIONS OF SHAKESPEARE PRIOR TO 1900 — Harold J. Nichols

FILM ADAPTATIONS OF SHAKESPEARE — Michael Anderegg, Department of English, University of North Dakota, Grand Forks, ND 58202

THE PRODUCTION OF SHAKESPEARE'S PLAYS IN NORTH AMERICA, 1875 to 1950: CONTEMPORARY PERSPECTIVES ON MODERN PRACTICE — Weldon Durham, Department of Theatre, University of Missouri, Columbia, MO 65211

SHAKESPEARE IN GERMANY AND EASTERN EUROPE — Ron Engle, Department of Theatre, University of North Dakota, Grand Forks, ND 58202

SHAKESPEARE IN THE ROMANCE AND SLAVIC LANGUAGES — Felicia Hardison Londré, Department of Theatre, University of Missouri-Kansas City, 5100 Rockhill Road, Kansas City, MO 64110

CONTEMPORARY PRODUCTIONS OF SHAKESPEARE IN THE U.S., 1946-PRESENT — Tice Miller, Department of Theatre, University of Nebraska, Lincoln, NE 68588

BRITISH PROUCTIONS OF SHAKESPEARE SINCE 1900 — Bob Schanke, Department of Theatre, Central College, Pella, IA 50219

Papers presented at the Theatre History Symposium will be considered for publication in *Theatre History Studies*.

## Mid-America Theatre Conference Award

The *Mid-America Theatre Conference* announces a $400 cash award for a graduate student research paper, to be presented at the 1984 MATC Theatre History Symposium on March 16-18 in Omaha, NE. The winning paper will be published in *Theatre History Studies*.

Oscar Brockett, University of Texas, Milly Barranger, University of North Carolina, and Richard Moody, Indiana University, will serve as the panel to select the winner. Brief written comments will be supplied to all entrants.

Send entries or inquiries to: Harold J. Nichols, Department of Speech, Kansas State University, Manhattan, KS 66506.